Man of a Certain Age: Making of a Happy Alcoholic

Living almost five decades brings a lot of joys, victories, losses, and heavy baggage to the mind. Every day.

Every day, the man you are about to know lived with many blessings and the counter-weight of regrets and indulgences, as too many middle-age men do.

This story is dedicated to those few blessings he knew and loved and who you will get to know through the coming pages. This written journey is also dedicated to the many men like him at that stage in life and, most of all, to the women who still love and support them…in spite of themselves.

Especially her…

And, it begins…..

Just imagine being born in a year of two historic and tragic assassinations, a war in Vietnam gone wrong, the beginning of free love & cultural revolution, and the election of one of the most narcissistic and disappointing American presidents in history. That's the world he was born into in mid-1968. He had no choice in the matter. He just entered the world around 3:30am that night. A small detail there, but maybe an indication as to how inconvenient he may become down the way…and may always be.

Childhood is as innocent as it gets, unless you grow up in the middle-class 1970's with pretty conservative parents and that centerpiece of their modest home, the television. One device in a big box that acted as that family's source of entertainment, information, and daily distraction from the mundane. Just bouncing all week, every week between church, school, and home - all week, every week - for an entire childhood can make one a bit odd. And, he was odd. Maybe it's hereditary. Yes, maybe genetic, or maybe his oddness is learned. Maybe, it's all of the above.

Two deeply Southern Baptist churches, two long-time, likable ministers, and two influential youth directors…like Noah, his emersion into organized religion came in two's. His church homes were a must to visit every Sunday morning and Wednesday night. Sure, it was about a solid, religious foundation, but it was about control, as well. It was also a getaway from the mundane at home and his father, a preacher's son, who only went to church for weddings and funerals. His father broke away from his mandatory religion that his dad preached and he never looked back. Another sign of things to come? Yes. Yes it was.

His family home was an ordinary rancher of the 1960's. 3 bedrooms and 2 baths with walls everywhere and a huge, rarely used living room and small kitchen-den combo that was the center of eating and entertainment. The walls were decorated with Guy Coheleach prints, gold-leaf framed mirrors, and his dad's crafty wooden decor. And, one phone from Ma Bell on the wall. A rotary dial phone with a 15 foot cord that would stretch all around the kitchen and conveniently to the comfy couch in the plush living room. There was a concrete patio out back, surrounded by dozens of tall pine trees and great old maples, those that are great for climbing and hiding. He hid in those a lot. Even when his mom, yelled out the kitchen window for dinner, he hid there. His backyard was huge, thanks for a utility line easement at the rear of the lot.

Kids were everywhere. His neighborhood, surrounded by two huge mountain ridges, sat in a valley that hugged those homes and families. Ranchers and split-foyers. Those were to norm and kind of separated the middle-class from the uppermiddle class folks. Ranch-style homes were simple and lessexpensive. His folks paid $16,000 for theirs and paid it off with $125 per month over 30 years. He can only dream about living in a two-story, luxurious split-foyer…near the neighborhood pool. Not with one, just near one. No one there owned their own pool, sans inflatable or plastic ones for the patio or yard.

Playdates did not really exist. Kids just ran the neighborhood at an early age. He cannot recall when, but it must have been when one gets their wheels in the form of a bike. Wandering off to neighbors' homes unannounced or just wandering off anywhere just happened….and no one freaked out. One was always just a corded, rotary phone call away. Just imagine, today, parents allowing their kids to just run the neighborhood at all hours of the day and evenings too. Bikes ruled. He eventually had and old cruiser with a banana seat. Not the coolest, but it was free and allowed for escape.

As for that pool…summers were hot and the pool was a savior. Best $100 family membership per year one could buy. Smallish pool, but with a deep end and a diving board. A little kiddie pool two for babies and toddler. He would eventually rule this domain in the years ahead as the sole lifeguard. He would also meet the bottom of the deep end and a way that still hurts to this day.

Next to the pool, there were two tennis courts that added a classy element to this neighborhood oasis. Tennis just seemed so sophisticated in such a community where high-school football ruled. Next to those courts were the community woods, where bike trails were many. So were hiding places for adult magazines that older boys stashed in tree stumps or wherever. His anatomical education began a bit early, thanks for those boys. Well, at least they were out side enjoying the great outdoors and bushes of all origins. Quite the shock and secret for such a Baptist soul…just the first of many, it seems.

Just imagine the last era of childhood void of gadgets, video games, handheld anything, any kind of personal, mobile phone, and cable television. One television with four channels. NBC, CBS, ABC, and PBS were it. And, it was actually fine. He did not know any different...yet. When not outside riding bikes, enjoying other neighbors collective riches, and just playing backyard sports, he was focused on PBS for Sesame Street, the Electric Company, and Mr. Rodgers and all of the big networks for evening entertainment. His third granddad seemed to stop by every weekday via CBS at 6:30pm. Walter Cronkite was his family's 24 minutes of connection to the bigger world and they watched him religiously during dinner everyday. ABC delivered afterschool specials and goofy celebrity-filled athletic competitions. NBC gave them Johnny Carson, Bob Hope special, and many other options. It was the golden era of variety shows. Carol Burnett & friends was the best. Flip Wilson, Mac Davis, Dean Martin and others were right up there too. Sports too. This week in Baseball with Mel Allen every Saturday and NFL football every Sunday and Monday night almost had the calendar covered. Howard, Frank, and Dandy Don on Monday Night Football was another getaway to look forward to every season. His teams were the Yankees, Lakers, and Cowboys, even though he had never been even close to NY, LA, nor TX. He just really like Reggie, Kareem, and Roger the Dodger and the teams the led very well. Oh, and mornings brought Captain Kangaroo and Casper the friendly ghost too. What's not to love over you homemade breakfast each day. Yes, his mom cooked meals all day. Not toaster or microwave anything. All year long. Every day. Homemade meals for breakfast, lunch at home or school, and dinner. They rarely ate out. It just didn't make economic sense and his mom was and is a darn good cook. And, she worked as a teacher's aide for nine months of the year too. Another era that seems to be a thing of the past.

As for getaways, his earliest memories consist of times at his paternal grandparents home, barber shop, and gardens and very rare vacations. Again, it was the 1970's and such simple times on a front-porch swing talking with neighbors, hanging out with a rotation of old men at his papaw's barber shop, and plucking really healthy food from the ground was always a treat. Who knew that you could grown your own healthy food behind the house and behind your business too? Back then, you just did. Must have been that surviving the Great Depression experience. Just guessing.

Escape outdoors or inside via great television was a must in the 1970's . Between Vietnam, Watergate, gas lines, incredible inflation, the Carter years, the hostage crisis, and the rise of terrorism against America…well, need he say more. Thank God for high-quality, limited-quantity entertainment options, including that new destination called the video arcade. Lots of quarters were spent in that den of real-life distraction. Tough decade to start a life…or was it? Looking back, he sees a simple era. Nightly television was a family affair. Kids played outside often and all day, all summer long. Bikes, trails, pools, basketball courts…as opposed to tablets, Wii, Xbox, iPods, etc. You created fun. It was rarely fed to you, except for that big box in the family den.

His dad brought home most of the proverbial bacon for his entire childhood and his mom literally cooked it. She even cooked up nightly snacks for them to enjoy during all of that must-see tv. The best of the best were the nachos. Grocery provided golden bliss warmed up and poured over crisp tortilla chips.

His dad made it through high-school, as his mom did. No college for them, just like their parents. That family tradition would be broken. His dad delivered newspapers with his dad and eventually on his bike, as a kid. He moved on to work at the local bakery, the same one that brought kids mini-loaves of fresh bread at school to sell their moms on that brand when grocery shopping. It probably worked quite well. Somehow, his dad moved on to a great sales job with Phillip Morris. Yes, he had a new marriage, first child on the way, and a new career in peddling cigarettes to store owners in every town and holler around this side of Appalachia. As is another new tradition, that success did not last and that shiny chrome, company car, and expense account had to be returned. He could have retired by his 50's or earlier, if peddling coffin nails remained acceptable. Oh, those potential stock options. Another sign of things to come, he recalls. This was the same man who was a star athlete and left home young to be a major-league pitcher. However, a rather large, black fellow sent a pitch back to him in Cincinnati and burned a real hole in the webbing of his baseball glove. He never really looked back. He just gave up. It's what men just do sometimes. No feel-good story there. A great deal of woulda-shoulda-coulda there and another sign for what he may have ahead for his life.

But, his came home, got a job, got married, bought a home, had a first boy, and played lots and lots of golf. His dad also bowled….really bowled…bowled and won. After he was born, his dad became the best bowler in town. He rolled one of the first 300's, a perfect game, in town. The diamond ring he won was huge and was better than any trophy. Too bad that his dad lost it decades later doing yard work . It was a really nice ring. Woulda. Shoulda. Coulda.

Then, that era ended as well. His dad was charged by the ABC, the governing body, with "blocking" the lanes of the bowling alley he then managed. All lanes have oil on them. But, if you poured that oil where a "pocket" for the ball was created and allowed for better scores and happier customers, well, that was against the ABC rules. His dad was fired and banned from bowling for something "everyone was doing" he was told. W. S. C.

His dad moved on to selling fire detection equipment and then Buster Brown shoes, whatever it takes. Then, the big settle. Just find that cozy corner where a job is guaranteed and wage increases and benefits and retirement are locks. His dad scored a steady job, so he thought, with a government contractor in the Secret City. Union Carbide and Martin Marietta and their work with nuclear waste became that family's new era, and would be so until his dad retired.

His dad's job was one of an "operator" who managed the recycling of spent nuclear material with others there in a highsecurity plant that also created the bombs that ended WW2 decades earlier. These plants had cool names like X-10 and Y-12 and his dad eventually worked in both over two decades or more. Those plants were now in control of his family's schedule for than any before. His dad, when enjoying sales and management jobs, escaped real family responsibilities by playing lots of golf when not working or sleeping. His older brother rarely saw his dad. His mom and dad almost did not make it through that era. His mom was a single-parent, more or less. His maternal grandmother stepped in and convinced his mom that this is just the way it is and stick with it. In this new, not-so Secret City era, his dad became a slave to the shiftwork of millions of dads and men around that decade who were just grateful for the "guaranteed" government-funded job. A constant reminder of this new era was taped to the inside of the main kitchen cabinet, the one that housed dished and glasses over the gigantic Panasonic microwave that still gets the job done 40 years later. I little checkerboard covered piece of paper that was coded in shades of gray and black and lines that told the family when dad would be gone or sleeping at home or maybe available to do family stuff. Guys working 8-hour shifts for day in different day-parts is a bitch. Just ask anyone who does it…or their sons.

Yet another reason why his dad slammed his life was to suggest that his boy do more with his life. So real. So sad, too.

Working holidays and overtime hours meant 150-200% boost in pay that day or two. Huge numbers for that family. The entire family knew what that meant. Extra food. Maybe eat out a little more. Maybe go somewhere. Who knows? His mom and dad were in that driver's seat. Kids had very little sway back then. His mom worked in a hospital years before and eventually scored a stable job as a teacher's assistant in the school's his bother and he would attend. Little pay, but summers off with her kids. It worked pretty well. She eventually worked her way up to be the "in-school suspension" person in his high-school. Kids, who get into trouble all of the time, loved her. They enjoyed being suspended and they tell her that to this day in the grocery store, at church, or wherever they still cross paths.

Suffice it to say, he had a solid, middle-class upbringing during a relatively economically and socially tough decade. He had all that he really needed and some things that he wanted. Another life lesson there that he would reflect upon as he gained and lost way too much "stuff". But, as a kid in that era, that polo with the little alligator meant so much. One shirt. It was yellow. The gator was over the left chest. His hair was feathered, just like the kid he wished was his best friend.

Then, there were Levi jeans. A must. Same for cool tennis shoes or loafers. Simple things kinda go with tough times. His dad's new lock of a career was shook up when layoffs hit and he went from his nuclear operator job to become a janitor in another plant there. He eventually worked his was back up to his former position with a new contractor and the road to retirement may just stay paved. As, for Alzheimers, well, the drone-like jobs cost his dad in other ways years later. That was his first decade's education from two parents who tough-loved, but also know when to laugh too.

They got it from somewhere. He barely knew his maternal grandparents until the end of his first decade. His granddad was a foreman for a steel company that built huge bridges around the mid-west and northeast. Bridges that almost everyone has driven across for flown over at some point on their trips. His maternal granddad was a steel man all the way. He gave and arm and almost a leg to the business. A pile of steel falling on you will do that. He never know him with two arms and that prosthetic are was one of the creepiest and crudest things he had ever seen. Needless to say, that are was rarely worn. But, that other arm was one of the strongest he had ever seen. When his grandparents retired, they came back to their home and finally became real grandparents. Cooky house with lots of hiding places and places to play. Cool neighbors. Toxic creek next to a huge garden that yielded food for many.

And, that brick incinerator where his granddad burned their trash and where they were both chased back home by a family of hornets that did not like the burn. His grandmother, Gigi, took care of everything in their home and shopped by bus or would allow her one-armed husband to drive her in their wood-paneled Country Squire station wagon. She never learned to drive, like many of their generation.

In his first 12 years, he does recall visiting these grandparents in two towns by air. Yes, his first plane trips were to Birmingham, Alabama and Lorraine, Ohio…but it was a plane to each and he had a new love. Those big steel tubes could maybe take you anywhere! This was new and fun. More to come about that down the road.

He fell in love with flying away then…to much better places than Backwards Ass Crossroads (BAC) and even the two places he had to go to see his grandparents. So many better places to come.

Once those grandparents moved back home, his real grandson life began with both sets of aging, but very active pairs of grandparents.

One set is retired and gardening. The other set has Papaw cutting hair six days a week and preaching on the 7th, while his grandmother takes care of their bungalow home.

Very Norman Rockwell, for that era. Both sets only live a couple of miles apart too and he was able to visit and spend the night with each often. Each have fun places to hang out, fun games to play, toys, and each were first to sign up for cable television. Watching live baseball from Atlanta and Chicago. Unreal! And movies on WTBS…Planet of the Apes…yes, please.

Most important gift from his extended family was what was sheltered and lived in those two old homes. Personality. Both couples were the same and different. All were kids of the depression. They knew what frugality and simple living was, but they each knew how to laugh. The kind of lose your breath kind of laughing. Pain in your side laughs. His Papaw even had a honk and a snort when he really laughed. He was a short, stout man who loved his wife's cooking. She was tall and bigger and sure could cook. She also had a "spshhhh" sound she would make in lieu of laughing loud. His Gigi was demure laughing, in order to prevent her teeth from popping out of her mouth. Her one-armed husband loved his Jim Beam, which was stored under the kitchen sink, and he had a gargle in his voice from imbibing with such, much to his Baptist daughter's chagrin. They all had personality, for sure.

They also had a fairly weird relationship with their kids, his parents. You had to go see them, more times than not. Hugs and kisses were in short supply.

Never travelled with them. Not once. His theory is that the house, garden, barber shop, and church were that nice, happy square mile that offered more daily satisfaction than the extended family experiences. But, it's just a theory and one he still motivates him to hug, kiss, and travel to and with his kids to this day.

And, he encourages their adventurous side at every turn, as he did not get anything close to that. His biggest grandparent adventures involved his Papaw showing him how to fetch a free grape Ne-hi out of the barber shop soda machine, picking okra from the garden, and maybe receive the coin stash from the same soda machine. That was about it. It was a pretty simple time, you know. Oh, and those trips to Papaw's with a sack full of Smokey Mtn Market hot-dogs, each with pre-ordered condiments and wrapped in paper. Another sweet, but salty, kinda redneck memory when visiting those grandparents…and he and his dad would compete over the number of dogs consumed…ah, quality time with dad.

As for holidays, those first years revolved around his paternal grandparents and his uncle and aunt's luxurious (for the 1970's), huge rancher with a basement. Thanksgiving and Christmas Eve were huge feasts and full of characters and personalities. Thanksgiving would have made Rockwell very proud. A feast. More food than necessary. A left-over bonanza for all to enjoy.

Big meal, a turkey-induced nap, NFL football (how 'bout them Cowboys?) and all of the smack talk about teams, pro and college, and just a good time, considering who was in the house. There was usually a bit of snoring too, during nap time, especially from his dad and his Papaw. No board games. No physical activity. No flag football nor shooting hoops. Just a huge meal, football on tv, and napping. It was bliss.

As for Christmas, the big highlight was Christmas Eve back at the same mansion of this particular family. They had a pool table in the sweet basement! And, a heated floor! A heated floor? How? It was magic, he guessed. They must be rich. Their home was triple the size of his. They only visited, or maybe were welcome, during the holidays. The home was decorated like a holiday village every time. It was perfect, in his eyes, and too much in his parents eyes…but they enjoyed those holidays, the meals, and the gift swap too. And, the smells. Seasonal candles were everywhere. And, that food. Yum. Except for the kids, there wasn't a single skinny family member, sans his own mom. This family ate very well. Just a bunch of well-fed, relatively happy people who only had to see each other two days a year. That seemed normal.

But, as they say, all good things do come to an end. It began with a village. It seemed to take a village. That terrible, ceramic village. The beginning of the the end came one Christmas Eve when they walked into that killer basement and found that the pool table was covered in felt and cotton and figurines and buildings that made for a simulated Christmas Village. It even extended past the edge and met the wall with a wooden structure that doubled the table size and simulated a mountainside too. It was depressing. No billiards that night. Priorities had changed. What's next? Cold floors? Gas insert in the big, stone fireplace? Take-out food? He would not be surprised. One night a year to shoot pool? Is that too much to ask? He thought not…the rest of that night is a blur.

His year-round existence was fairly self-made, from birth to 12 years of age. Sports were not a passion, but a boredom killer. He played baseball, but not very well. One, single home-run in his little league career was his lone highlight. One ankle-high pitch that allowed for his golf swing homer to dead center field. One and only one homer trot. That's really all he needed. But, he loved watching baseball and collecting player cards. With his dad's help to collect and his summer mowing money, his collection grew from a few to over 15,000 in individual collector cards and full sets of cards. He would also look forward to his monthly haggle with one Mr. Martin, a school principal who loved to deal with anyone at his flea market booth. Mr. Martin loved dealing with kids and deal they did. He was a joy to wheel and deal with.

As for other sports, he played basketball and he and his dad put up a regulation goal between his dad's wood-shop, the stack of firewood, and the laundry clothesline. It was a grass court, for a while. It was where we grew calves on his legs to huge proportions. Constantly jumping for hours will do that. He played league basketball too, where he was large and incharge at low post. Never guard nor forward material. This is back when there was an actual "center" position, which seems to have disappear as all players now are huge. Kareem Abdul Jabbar was the man and his favorite player on his favorite Laker team. He emulated and practiced his "sky hook" at every turn. Too bad the coaches frowned upon such successful moves.

Football was never a consideration and won't be for his boys. Maybe that comes from the football addiction crazy community he's determined to get away from someday.

His "sport", if you can call it than back then, was golf. This was back in the days where golfers and bowlers were mostly fat guys and bigger ladies who enjoyed the leisure, the beer, smoking whatever you like, and riding around chatting for hours. That was golf, before personal trainers, work-outs, and health concerns. But, thanks to 8mm film, he can recall rather skinny parents and friends vacationing, before he was born, in Florida with other skinny friends…men with crewcuts and women with bouffant hairdo's and baby oil for suntanning. Those were the skin cancer-be-damned days.

His dad took up golf in his successful 30's and played 6-7 times a week when he manage bowling lanes at night. His dad also prided himself about the fact that he was the poorest shmuck at that particular country club and other members let him know it. But, he paid his dues and no snob could stop him from playing daily between sleep and bowling lane management. Not much of a considerate father and husband back then, but they managed.

Golf was both recreation and entertainment. His dad somehow always had the cash to play and to take his son with him whenever he could. He understood this about his dad and took every opportunity to learn and enjoy the game with him. He was also able to play with the saltiest dogs on terra firma. They all cussed like sailors, especially a little guy named Kyle and an old coot named Roy. They love hanging out with his dad and took him in as a kid pal on the public links. He was able to improve his game while enjoying his dad and pals having fun too. Can guy time get any better when your a kid? Apparently not. He was not the focus. No team to impress. Just old farts and a kid in the fresh air, poking fun, and laughing at each other for a few hours. Golf was his ultimate father-son connection like none other. Golf demands respect, manners, efficiency, and time….lots of time each outing. Driving to and from the course and playing would be a 5-6 hour experience. Lots of time to chat, listen, and learn. To this day, although he hasn't played in years, his golf grip of each club (called a "baseball" grip) is what his dad taught him. No pro golfer uses such a grip. So contrarian…and he'll go right back to it when the time is right and sons-in-law or grandkids want to play the game with him. He could still rip it, but lacks the desire and motivation to get out there. Burnout is another factor, as you will learn later.

Golf is a spoiled man sport today. Too expensive for a decent course. damn balls. Too expensive to gear up. Too expensive for

He remembers a day when free golf balls were everywhere…or where he could find them. Used balls for cheap were also around. His dad is gone now and so is the will to play a game that he remembers fondly. His love of playing the sport kinda died with his dad a few years ago, and he's fine with that. Too many wonderful memories to relive on any given course. Maybe other loved ones will motivate his game again someday.

As the 1980's kicked into gear, this family of 3, with a grown and absent older brother focused on simple getaways that they could afford in time and money. All 3 shared a few loves…the beach, tasty food, and getting away from it all… even for one week a year. That was it. Remember the middle class. They used to be huge. The engine for a nation. Good times. Good times.

Anywho. His family of 3 was the middle. If his dad's bonus came prior to summer, the family paid as they went to the Atlantic coast. If not, his mom would visit the local teachers' credit union and borrow the $1k or so needed for that one week of getaway, in AMEX travelers cheques, of course. Never cash. It's just safer…and you know it.

Let's back up just a bit. His first beach experience timed out well with the most dramatic beach blockbuster ever. "Jaws" hit the theaters right before his first recalled beach trip. He was 6 or so and could not see the movie. But, there was a funny neighbor was nice enough to share the info and warn the young child about how to avoid a shark attack. Very nice. However, as a pretty rational child, he somehow knew that Jim was "pulling his leg" (a frequent local colloquialism). Everyone around him seem to do that from time to time. After all, only yankees up north could be eaten. The movie proved that. However, just in case, even as a child, he would make sure that, every time he entered the salty water, he would stay slightly inside the imaginary, parallel line from the beach. Others would surely be eaten before him. It just made perfect sense. That was his first beach love experience at the place they still refer to as Myrtle Beach. His first beach experience also includes an epileptic seizure en route.

Nothing like swallowing your tongue to really set the vacation mood. His dad pulls the family truckster over on a little highway somewhere in South Carolina and his mom plunges her index finger into his little pie hole. Done. Thanks to those handy drugs called Dialanton and Finabarb, life moved on for a while.

Once there, his beach experience continued. Forty years ago, beach experiences were just different. They were only a week long. His family experience revolve completely around lots of sun, sand, and seafood. Keeping it simple was the annual plan. Find that cheap motel on the beach, hit the sand early everyday, and get to the early bird dinner with less traffic and wait. Sleep and do it all over again. Sure, puttputt (miniature golf) was a must too, as was real golf as he got a little older. But, laying on and walking the beach for miles and body surfing the waves were as much sport as this little boy needed. He would pretend to be various superheroes too, as he crushed or avoided each colossal 2-3 foot wave. had a proven way to deal with that burning sun. They also

Just burn. One good burn and the Solarcaine and air conditioning combo that night would set you up for a killer tan the remaining week. SPF 70? Really? No such thing. His mom believed in the good, first burn to set up the remainder of the summer. He recalls sunscreen in the form of SPF 2 Hawaiian Topic and/or Coppertone Oil...oh, that wonderful smell.

Not of burning flesh, but that oil. That wonderful coconut-infused smell. Myrtle Beach just turned into Maui with that oil. Another future sign of beach love to come...Maui. Love.

Fry. Then cool. That was the way. Thank God for the big window air conditioner at the Caribbean hotel that cooled the Solarcaine slathered burn. No joke. Fry and cool was in.

Much like the seafood they enjoyed. Okay, lotsa solid skin cancer in their future. Years later, his parents had plenty of little things burned or frozen off to prevent a faster death. It worked. He's headed that way too, thanks to his mom's burn theory and his lifelong love of the sun and sunny places. There are worst ways to go, he thinks.

Moving on. Then, there was Hawaii. Not the real one. Just a contrived version near their home in a tourist trap town near the mountains. Porpoise Island was it's name. Just imagine a Hawaiian village, hula girls, and rides in the Smokies. Unreal, but very real to him. Picture an oasis of lush tropical landscapes and all one could imagine of a place over 5,000 miles away. His folks could never afford such a trip to the real Hawaii, so their brief experiences at this faux Hawaii would have to do. And, it did. Ironically, his and Love would someday honeymoon on Maui, celebrate an anniversary there, and use lots of Delta Skymiles to send his and her parents there on separate trips to Maui. Trips of their lifetimes, he thinks.

Getaways growing up, as you can tell, were simple, but fun. Beaches and mountains. That's about as exotic as they were. All reachable by car. And, that was just fine with him. Anywhere away from the usual was epic.

As for the mountains, there was always great "people watching" in Gatlinburg and close by in Silver Dollar City. And, there was Ghost Town in the Sky. Cowboys killing each other after you took a sky lift up to this mountain top town in the sky. A town with no law. A town where city slickers aren't welcome. A town where well-scripted gun slingers would scream at each other and shoot faux ammo until each were not really dead. As goofy as it get and he loved it.

Enough about fun. Then, there was that school.

Preschool at a local Baptist church, of course. Then, on to elementary school and his catholic nun-like teacher, Ms. Corum. She ruled her roost with great force and intimidation, as he recalls four decades later. Old, gray, and tough she was. Maybe she was only 50 or 60, but she seemed old to a little boy.

His first day was tough, but, cue the music…preferably "Dream Weaver"…there she was. Beth. Perfect Beth. He was smitten for the first time ever. Her hair was made of pure gold. Her beauty set the stage for his love of blonde beauties for his lifetime. This first love was never mutual, but did last for their entire 12 years of schooling in that hometown. Even when a new elementary school was built and split them up for three years, he kept that internal boy flame going. He had fallen in unrequited love and it was wonderful.

Fortunately, there were more sweet little girls. Becky lived in his neighborhood and had another posh split-foyer with a pool table downstairs. A great kissing spot for little kids. Who knew? And, Leslie, who liked to kiss and hug a lot. All were sweet, special, and his love for a time. But, life is short when you're in elementary school.

Most of all, don't be fooled by all of that action. He never saw action like that until after graduation and into his freshman year of college. Well, his high school Senior Trip to, again, Myrtle Beach, saw a little action.

Very little. Digressing a bit here, but it's good. Just a fortunate little boy grew into a goofy young boy and man with zero interest from good girls (but with interest from three experienced, scary ones). In short, there was a huge chasm between 1974 and 1986 when it came to romance. That's where a little thing like technology came in like manna from

Heaven.

It started with video arcades where lots of time and quarters were blown. Then, his family acquired "Pong", his first and very rudimentary , black and white video game that was revolutionary and more than boring.

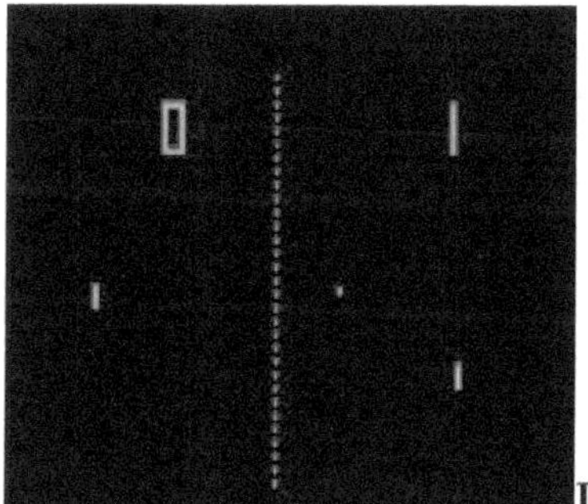Imagine such a world today where video ping-pong or digital tennis seemed riveting.

That tan and faux wood paneled box delivered its goods via two little brass or copper clips that one could actually connect with screws built into the back of any give television. Yes, tv's has actually screws on the back to attach rabbit ear antennas and new video game consoles. Pong was a gamechanger for them. And, just the beginning. It was like creating the first technological wheel for home consumption. It was no comparison to those dozens of cool video games waiting for all at the local arcade, which are now mostly extinct. He could spend hours there, until the quarters ran out, bouncing between Donkey Kong, Tetras, Galactica, Qbert, PacMan, et al.

Outside of Pong, back at home, there was one other guaranteed way to escape the normal, and it's still there in his mom's home today. One huge Magnavox stereo that played records and also auto-tuned in radio stations. It was a huge piece of console furniture that was to the plush living room what the television was to the tiny den. It not only played records and tuned in the radio on the right side, it stored one hundred or more records (Dean Martin, ABBA, Journey, Boston, Chicago, Jim Croce, Beach Boys, and many others) on the left side of the open console. One big, heavy, wooden console that entertained and looked pretty impressive too.

It will be a dream come true for his friend named Jim who likes to tinker with such 50+year old treasures. Someday.

Past the technology and needed distractions of that era, there were a couple of highlights of this boy's elementary school career. He played Oz in the Wizard of Oz production, since he had a low voice and some dramatic flair. That was fun. And, best of all, he wrapped up his year as a Safety Patrol with a trip to Washington D.C.. An amazing trip. One he had never experienced with other kids and without his parents. It was his Senior Year of elementary school and they were going to party like it was 1979. They were the first graduating class of the new, temporary school down the street from his home. That school is still there, 40 years after it was built. His trip was epic, since they could run the National Mall with no supervision. They were just told to travel in buddy groups and be back at a certain time. Freedom. Fun. No adults watching over them. Those days must be gone by now. Replaced with headcounts, group tours, and maybe GPS tracking devices in everyone's underwear.

Not only did he get to go. He went with his new love, his teacher. They shared a last name. It must be kismet. Alas, she had wooed the local, mobile home magnate away from his first wife and married him. They sang jingles on his tv commercials. He just focused on his WSJ en route and love lost. However, running that town was good medicine.

A new era...... There it was. That shining light on a hill. That was the way one man envisioned a renewed America. Malaise was the current President's view of America. He seemed hopeless and worn out from the job. The 444 daily newscasts leading with the hostage crisis in Iran was the last nail in the decades presidential coffin. It was great to see all of it go and be replaced by hope and pride in America's potential. Even as the new leader of the free world was being sworn into office, the 53 hostages were boarding a plane to return home. It seemed that the changing of leadership instantly changed the perception of those in Iran about America

At home, his family's hope and optimism took a big jump

too. Both parents worked while he spent summers mowing yards for a few years and eventually lifeguarding at the neighborhood pool. His dad did have a few mishaps at work that required trips to the local hospital. When things blow up in a recycled nuclear waste plant, well, things can get burned. Things like one's skin, even through protective suits. No fuss. No lawsuits. His dad was just happy to have a good-paying job. His mom was too. And, she enjoyed being in the middle- and high-school atmosphere, kids, and staff. His schools. She eventually worked her way into a position of supervising inschool suspension, where he fortunately never found himself. Others, though, loved her wit and strict ways and did not mind being her room doing desk work all day during their suspension. He believed some kids got in trouble on purpose to get out of their usual classes. His mom was gifted in toughlove and it seemed some really needed it.

In this new era, his world was about to change for the better again. As I write this, Microsoft turns 40 years old today. Little did he know what that meant to him and the world. Let alone Apple, Intel, and, much later, Google. Here comes his first personal computer, the Commodore 64. Yes, 64k with an external cassette tape hard drive. It spoke in DOS. His school had no such thing. But, one Christmas morn, he had his. It cost $400 and would introduce him to programming and entertainment past television. But, there was no monitor nor a mouse, as he recalls. Just a fat keybord/CPU that plugged into his tv and corded to the external hard drive. He programmed in his baseball card collection and saved the data to his cassette tape. So archaic, but just the beginning. An Apple or Mac back then was too expensive. The Commodore fit the bill and was that one killer Christmas present that year. He became a young programmer and he loved that new world. DoS was terribly complicated and allowed for zero errors to achieve the programming goal. But, it seemed important and exciting. Where was this technology going next? He found that pretty inspirational.

He had no pets, no siblings for the most part, and was left to his own devices to entertain himself most of the time. The Commodore did just that, much like handheld gadgets for kids today. Just like Pong, which is in storage somewhere now, the Commodore will eventually end up in some funky museum somewhere that displays historic technologies.

Then, the next Christmas, home video games were ready to explode. There was Atari, Intellivision, and ColecoVision. He was a fan of the last. Cool, black console with large paddle, joy sticks with keypads and those chunky game cartridges. Donkey Kong came with the console. How sophisticated it was, relative to Atari. Intellivision was cool but too expensive.

The era of little and big boys held up in their room for hours at a time had begun. Being outside was still a must, but it took a hit when Santa dropped new technologies under the tree. As baseball and basketball lost their luster for him, he was left to his waves of technology bliss indoors and just golf outdoors.

He loved golf. He and his dad tried to fish together, but golf was something both really enjoyed. They played fairly often over the coming years. Golf became the thing to do on days off, which came in 2-3 days off at a time, between shifts at the plant. Public courses only, since the budget did not allow otherwise. They were members for years between two great country clubs, but could not budget the expense about the time he was old enough to swing a golf club. So, they played a rotation of several decent courses, no matter how far they needed to drive his dad's truck. The chartreuse Toyota truck was the first ride and then came the much bigger GMC later.

Those years of playing golf with his dad and his dad's old friends were special. Those old guys smoked. They cussed. They all poked fun at one another. And, they all loved his mom and could not understand how his dad married such a woman. Real men near the end of their respective careers getting outside and having their social time together for a few hours on weekends, busting each others chops over golf.

He really liked those 4-5 hour experiences and his mom probably enjoyed the break too.

As the economy recovered from a recession, the family's fortunes improved and a decent retirement for his folks seemed more likely. It was a decent, middle-class existence. (Although, years later, his first wife would enlighten him to the fact that they were lower middle-class compared to her upper-middle class family. Another sign of things to come… maybe another reason why she was just a practice marriage.)

Life moved on quite nicely for them, during the Reagan Revolution. Heading into puberty, things did get a lot better Revolution. Heading into puberty, things did get a lot better track tapes, records, and cassettes to cable tv, CD's, video games, and what seemed like permanent preservation of shows and movies via an RCA brand of VCR (with a corded remote control). That was his next big Christmas gift. A big box that could record anything on television and let you watch anything over and over! Revolutionary! Great movies, comedy specials, sports, mini-series, and lots of sit-coms were in his library. And, it was a video library. Racks and racks of VHS tapes, never BetaMax. Unbelievable. He went from programming computer code to a gamer to programming his on television entertainment, all within a couple of years. This tech savvy GenX generation was just getting started and his parents could not really understand it yet…until, his dad started his own video collection of old westerns, golf, and other things he liked a lot, but may miss while at work.

The Transition
All kids seem to grow up too fast, especially to their parents…unless they give them pain…then, well…

He gave his parents very little trouble. He watched his much older brother be a huge pain for both parents and even his little brother. He could not wait to see his brother leave, then he returned, and left again. His brother was practically a PhD in how not to be a son, husband, father, and brother. In other words, another former stud and jock with a Napoleon complex that translated into nothing productive over the long-term.

He learned priceless skills from his much older brother in how to speak to and treat your parents for greatest success with daily life needs and the rare big ones. His parents returned the favor by working hard to give him as many opportunities to grow and learn as they could afford.

His Baptist upbringing added a little boost to his parents' moral and ethical lessons. He had a very, healthy fear of consequences, reaffirmed over and over again by his older brother. At school, he performed well with almost all A's & B's his entire educational career. Not perfect, like him, but good enough in every grade to please and impress.

This boy began with not much of a competitive bone in his body and that never really changed, from academia to sports to keeping up with any Joneses. Never competitive, but he sure liked nice things from a very young age.

What he may have lacked in academic perfection and in athletic prowess, he tried to make up for in personality and character. His earliest memory of this is when he hammed it up with high school cheerleaders as a little boy and they went nuts over his long eyelashes. He was a cute kid, even with a burr haircut. But, those baby blue eyes and long lashes, he discovered a good thing there. Maybe that was the beginning of his thing for blondes & cheerleaders, preferable blonde cheerleaders. He was pretty helpless there. Posters of Farrah Fawcett and the Dallas Cowboy Cheerleaders covered his bedroom walls. Classic...

Hormones. Pure hormones drive the transition from a boy to young man.

This was his big transition in the 1980's and the wonderful and crushing distraction of girls pretty much took over. He grew up watching old-school guys like Sinatra, Dean, Carson and even Flip Wilson win over their audiences with humor first and then style. He would never quite get there in the debonair style category, but humor he could do. He could even use humor to not only entertain, but to cover up his mundane life. Never a stud nor able to dress to impress, he fell back on pleasing others with high-shock factor humor. He also learned that from his dad, who cracked people up all the time by saying what many think, but would never speak. That earned him fairly frequent smacks across the arm from his mom, their resident Baptist backbone. His parents' friends and even strangers were always commenting on their youngest son's maturity and humor. That was better than any report card.

By 7th grade, the fitting-in thing finally hit the wall. Until then, he was a me-too, a tag-along, a sad sight for such a smart and insecure little guy. But, he was growing. Tall and skinny and not popular at all. More girl friends (no romance) than guy friends by a bunch. But, there was one friend he just wanted to be. Blue eyes were about all they had incommon. He had that perfect, blonde, and feathered hair all of the girls loved. Throw in his own personality and sense of humor and he just had it all.

He knew and followed his long-time pal whenever he could. Until, that day came. He cannot recall the argument, the fight, the kerfuffle that provoked their teacher to take action. He cannot even recall their teacher's name. But, he left an impression or two. This come-to-Jesus sit-down with their teacher was shocking and tense, but ended with their teacher lecturing his pal about how cool he may think he is, but how his lesser friend will leave him in his wake someday. They were both stunned, in different ways. What teacher lays down a firm judgement like that? A frustrated one, it seemed. That was one helluva tipping point for him. He now has at least one who offer a passionate case to stand alone and run with life, not follow others. A few harsh words from one teacher one afternoon seemed to do more for his self-esteem than 12 years of parenting. Funny how life works that way.

(BTW, both boys grew up to eventually marry their true loves, find success, and have wonderful children)

Fast-forward 30+ years…and his 10-yr old boy advises him that he plans to be an engineer and use that skill in the U.S. Navy. He nodded and encouraged his boy to take the next 10 years or so to research and figure that out. To which his boy replies, "Actually, dad, my teacher says that we should know what we want to do with our lives by 4th or 5th grade." Another teacher leaving her notch in a boy's brain.

When he was a young boy, he knew that he wanted to be an airline pilot. Yep. Just knew it, like his boy did decades later. He sent off for a brochure and application to EmbryRiddle Aeronautical school in Florida. They arrived and he was pumped, albeit a decade or so too soon. He has initiative, for sure. Then, it hit him that flying all over the world as a commercial pilot would be fun…but…he could have much of a home life with a wife and kids. Yes, even as a kid, he worried about not being there for his family, as needed. Weird. His dream quickly died. FBI? Same thing. The government could send those agents anywhere for any amount of time and no one may know where you are. FBI dream gone too. Again, his dad missed a lot of family time and maybe that's where his fear began. This old soul began to live a bit, it seemed.

He wanted a nice home, with a sunken den and woodburning fireplace, all for a happy family that would have the ability to entertain each other and many others over decades to come. He eventually had that in several very different homes. To get there, he vowed to not settle for a desk job, no mundane job, nothing like what a high-school diploma delivers. It must be more. He was a young entrepreneur mowing lawns, up to 18 lawns 1-2 times per month. Thousands of dollars per season. Where did it all go??? He enjoyed the flexibility , negotiation, and the satisfaction of getting paid for a needed service. Maybe that was in his career future… and it was.

That first entrepreneurial taste began by posting flyers in the neighborhood, riding the mower to each customer while dragging the push mower and weed eater behind him, then moved on to partnering with a pal down the street to service other neighborhoods. With two, they were more productive too and that VW wagon, middle seat removed, carried all week needed. Once that pal moved on, his did was more than willing to pick up the need and help him travel, as needed, in the old GMC truck. His dad even built to long ramps to ride the mower up in the bed of the truck. He would ride while his dad would trim the yards. His dad even let him keep the money he earned, just as his granddad did when driving his dad around every morning delivering newspapers, decades earlier.

It was hard work, but paid well with up to 18 yards mowed over 5-6 months. And, the money was blown on who knows what. Spending money on vacation, clothes, baseball cards, video games, for sure. It was the first of several financial miscues in his first-half lifetime. He realizes now that it really does pays to have a financial mentor…it's even more valuable when one is willing to listen to said mentor. He had neither a mentor nor such listening skills. Maybe, it was hereditary. One day, his folks travelled up to a local, tourist trap town and took a tour of a small timeshare complex. When they returned, they were $4,500 lighter in savings, but they had one annual week to bargain with and they also had a free country ham. "Free" or $4,500 ham, depending on your perspective. A trip to the meat market may have offered a much better ROI. Live and learn…or not. However, there week was traded annually for weeks in other places that were much nicer. His folks were able to enjoy different vacations for about 25 years. That week is up for sale now. And, in a last twist of flimflam , the sale of a timeshare week demands that the seller pay the buyer up to $2,000 to take it off her hands. So, the buyer is also a seller, of sorts. Fair warning, timeshare prospects out there.

As middle school chugged along and high-school was fast approaching, another change was needed. He and his mom had attended an old Southern Baptist church near the first home his mom and dad had bought thirty years ago. Most of his friends and acquaintances attended on of two neighborhood churches much closer to their current home of many years. One was a dying church. The other was a church full of families and familiar faces. His mom acquiesced and they made a meaningful leap to their new church. He was a leader in the old youth group, had let a youth newsletter effort (His favorite editorial was "Would Jesus wear a Rolex?"), and he even challenged church leadership in his editorials, which did not go over too well. He would be starting over and he was grateful for his mom's willingness to change. Very grateful.

Life just seemed to plod along, like it does for most people. Those awkward middle school years were ending and another summer approaches. And, that very summer between middle school and high school brings his little scruffy city the World's Fair. This dingy, dusty little downtown had virtually died, thanks to suburbia and the move westward to live, shop, and play. This downtown had almost died. Then, a savvy banker and his politician had an idea and they made it happen. President Reagan came to open up the Fair. It was a summer of 11 million visitors coming into town and enjoying what was the greatest tourist event in downtown ever. Dingy and drab went to lively and like a Disney destination, as much as it could be in a temporary way. The park remains, as does the iconic Sunsphere building/tower/gold golf ball in the sky. He went as much as the family would take him. Very fond memories of that summer and fall of 1982. Having never been out of his country , this brief event offered a slight glimpse into other countries and cultures, which he could not really appreciate for years to come.

Again, all good things must come to an end. And, boy, did it ever. The Fair closed at the end of October and it's founder's home was stormed the next morning by the local FBI. Front page news, of course. He was a crooked banker and he eventually went to jail. It was during that crazy S&L era. He was also a presumptive candidate for Governor, after a successful Worlds Fair. Not anymore. Many locals lost their savings.

Fortunately, his folks had their money with another local bank that remains as solid today as ever. As a bonus, the neighbor who gave him the idea to be an FBI agent was on the front page of the paper, raiding the lakeside home of the fallen banker and his wife. Whirlwind was its name and seems to be more than apropos. The estate was sold off and is now a bunch of condos. Live and learn, crooked bankers.

Real loss. A first for the boy.

The worst kind of loss was coming. The only grandmother who was their on Cambridge Ave. his entire life was losing hers. The woman who kept a "cuss box" on her dresser and it always had change in it. The woman who always seemed to have three fresh, buttermilk biscuits under a lid and on the stove ready to him to eat. The woman who taught him how to garden and hang wet laundry up in the breeze. The woman who introduced him to the sweet ride of a 1968 Olds, like riding a cloud, on the way to Emery's 5&10 and Krystal for lunch. The wife of a preacher/barber who played marbles with him on the living room carpet and tucked him into that third bedroom when he came to sleepover. Now, that third bedroom was her deathbed. Cancer laid there too. Breast cancer, to be exact. Surgery must have happened, but it wasn't discussed. She was just sick. That's all that mattered. Her spirits were great. Her wigs were fine too. She had pride. Always. Like his mother's "under the weather" or hysterectomy, I just we folks just don't discuss such things as a family. (That would change with his family.) He can still recall his grandmother moving from her large, front bedroom to the middle one. Papaw slept in the back bedroom, behind the kitchen. It's what they did. Her bed could raise and lower with a touch of a button. And, to this day, he cannot look at that bumpy foam that prevents bedsores without thinking of her. And the smell of cedar... her cuss box was made of cedar. There were burned on instructions that told you just how much to put in that box for what level of profanity. Such a funny dresser decoration for a preacher's wife, don't you think? It was funny, but just a simple distraction from the long goodbye he and his family were living that year or two. Death never seemed to be an issue, but it became one then. His last greatgrandparents died around the time he was born. This was his first great loss. A horrible first. Watching one you love waste away at home and go from one tough woman to withered and pain-filled is terrible. He was overdue, it seemed. He had never really experienced loss and here it was. Maybe at the right time, where he could appreciate it. Maybe. But, she eventually succumbed to that horrible cancer. She was gone, along with his dad's image. His dad never said "I Love You" to him or anyone he can recall. His dad kept some kind of image or persona going at all times. However, in that limo, behind that hearse, his dad lost it. His Papaw lost it. And, he followed and lost it too. Three generations losing it together. Never did tears flow like that in his presence…the first of a few more to come. She was a tough woman and her husband, son, and grandson were anything but tough that day. But, what a memory. He was seemingly the right age to learn of such loss. God works in weird ways that way. It prepared him, just a bit, for more losses to come.

Middle school may be tough, but it's nothing compared to the 4-year pressure of fitting in and succeeding in some form before launching into college…which is a must. No one in his immediate family had made it through college. That must change.

He went into his next to last educational era with his mom there running in-school suspension and everyone knew her and seemed to love her. Don't screw up, kid. Granted, he had kept his nose clean since 2nd grade, when he chose to refer to his teacher by her first name, Kay, since his mom knew her. Big mistake. He never forgot that bad day at the age of 7.

He was damn determined to impress his folks, work smart, but not too hard, and do whatever it takes to get the hell out of BAC ASAP, where football wins meant more than a quality education and any cultural growth whatsoever. Sadly, his youth shown through with a systematic disdain for the most artistic group at his school, the Madrigals. Music, theatre, and dance, all together. A sad regret on his part. He would have been great, if the homophobic tendencies back then could have been suppressed. It was the early 1980's and any guy in tights might just be a victim of AIDS. It was a stupid, ignorant, and scary time. No straight kid would dare get to close to those artistic ones who might carry that gay disease. Hard to comprehend that now, but it was just that way in that corner of the world.

Ironically, he would grow up to love Broadway, offBroadway, Off-off-Broadway, and their road shows…and even little productions in his little downtown. And, he certainly grew to resent his prejudice and ignorance of that time, which maybe robbed him of an artistic career or at least hobby to pursue. Maybe he can still be a character actor in his sunset years. We shall see. Ten years later or so, he was another guy.

Transforming from a smart boy to a smarter young man was fairly rapid. High school can be brutal. In a lilly white school of sheltered ones, poor to quite wealthy, it was and is not a healthy American experience. All of the parents & kids were white. All of the teachers were white. All of the administrators are, you guessed it, were white. Not quite the real world. Oops, he did have a Korean-American friend. He was hilarious. And, there was that one tall girl that was bi-racial. That was his multicultural experience in that little community. Sadly, he thought at the time that this was just the was it was everywhere, except in those big cities where riots, looting, fires, and common muggings and thuggery just reigned over all. Cronkite reported it. It must be true.

Sure, they had a cross-burning in someone's yard once or twice…doesn't everyone? No? Oh. Well. It must have been more Christian to keep the community pure and discourage those of color from moving north of town. After all, east of town had lot of those folks and the powers that be were historically determined to keep it that way.

Most in his community were good people and had no knuckle-dragging interests. But, few stepped up to right the wrongs of that time and he slowly learned about the bigger, wonderful, artistic, open-minded, and inclusive world out there. It took travel and a higher educational experience.

He was stuck, like he would be a few times down the road. But, stuck in a small community with no live theatre, no live jazz, no culinary experiences, no real arts of any worth. Just fast food, buffet restaurants, strip malls, used car lots, and high school football. No real culture to mention. Just small town nothing…and a golf course. Hence the importance of escape via that big box in the den. Television and its escape just jumped in importance. Watching "Dallas" on Friday night was a cultural highlight. If football or something else got in the way, pop that mega-cassette in the VCR and let that RCA do the job for you.

But, he did have sports, so to speak. He made the freshman basketball team, but the coach was a little odd. His coach liked to watch the boys dress in the locker room. Not normal. His first pervert epiphany had occurred. He also returned to golf. He lettered all four years, but never bothered with one of those vinyl, gaudy jackets. Golf is not quite a sport, anyway. It's a luxury. It's a lilly white , non-impact game where it just feels good to be outside on perfectly manicured lawns where one can feel wealthier than they probably are. No downside there, for a middle-class kid. He was the only non-member of his school's home course. His family had been a member there. His folks had played there and sunned poolside there. His brother had played golf and bet himself into a hole there. It just seemed like another faux home to him. He loved the game that his dad taught him. Loved it. Hated it sometimes too. But, on the team, there were free golf balls every match. Gotta love that.

His dad taught him the grip, swing, and art of playing a decent round of golf. He also shared a few indecent and racist things too. Things that haunt him still today. Brazil nuts. Simple. They're just nuts. Big, dark, tasty nuts. To him… nigger toes. Yep. He still avoids the mixed nut section of the grocery store to this day. Cashews, almonds , and pistachios, please…but, no mixed nuts, thank you. It's automatic and sad. See anyone of dark color in the hot summer sun "sweating like a nigger"…yep, he cannot help it to this day. It was said in jest way back then and he still sadly recalls it every time. His mom's slapping of his dad could not slap away the tasteless reference and his memory of such negativity. Okay. Bigotry. Racism. Those connotations still stick with him today. Sad, don't you think? Moving on…

As everyone probably knows, high school is quite the huge first right of passage into young adulthood. It's where his hormonal years really kick in. He's an over-achiever, but it only really scores points with teachers and other adults. It gets him nowhere with the girls. He never had a girlfriend. Never. Just friends who happen to be girls and a few friends who happened to be guys. Maybe this was all by design. Maybe God wanted him to avoid the drama and save his emotions for the triumphs and tragedies to come down the road. Maybe.

His freshman year began after his first year as lifeguard at his neighborhood pool. A great teenager job and it paid a little money too. No more mowing everyday. Just slather up, test that water, and watch over the little kids and very cute girls & their moms alike. This was the same pool where he popped off his top two teeth on the bottom of the deep end of the pool. Diving off the diving board with his arms by his side and misjudging the bottom rising…pop…his teeth were snapped off. It still hurts him to think about that today. Those 30+ year temporary teeth are still firmly in place.

He was fast-developing into a young man. Somewhat handsome, in that 1980's big hair and skinny mustache sort of way. You probably don't see it. Neither did the young ladies of that era. So, what do you do? Evidently, you try out for the golf team. And, you make it. His dad was nowhere in sight and his new golf partners were teammates and strangers. Their home course was the very country club where his parents dropped out as he just started swinging a club. They just couldn't afford it. Little did he know that he would afford a membership for the entire family someday. Lots of golf, meals, and libations there down the road. But, for now, he was a freshman on the golf team and was new to the level of joking and extremely foul language coming from the older guys. Skinny Lenny and the foul-mouthed Rick. They led the team that year. Wow. It was quite the fall season.

He also made the freshman basketball team, but golf was outdoors, did not smell awful, and did not require banging up against smelly, sweaty dudes all afternoon. He just loved being outside in fresh air and that never changed. He made the junior varsity team the next year and hated it. He was done with basketball. He wasn't a shooter, just a bruiser. Need someone to foul, he was your guy. Need someone to score, not so much. Golf was his thing. Not an adequate replacement for girls, but it would have to do.

Academically, he was on it. Not an over-achiever determination. Just a work-smart, not hard ethic strategy that became his life-long constant. And, that began very early in his life. Sure, there were AP classes. But why? He had no Ivy League or like ambitions. He just wanted to go to college. Any college would do. His family bar was set very low.

He did not buy into the obsession with football and basketball seasons. He was one of the majority of boys who never made it past the on-deck circle or the bench or the sidelines in their chosen sport. He was determined not to be sidelined, benched, or left on-deck through his life.

Mr. and Miss high school that freshman year were a stud football guy and a gorgeous cheerleader neighbor of his. Pretty typical and perfect. Again, little did he know that he would be there with his first love, perfect Beth, just a few years later.

Funny now. This beautiful, little girl of 5 grew up to be a beautiful young lady with zero interest in him. But, the faux union would happen in a few years.

Back to reality. Remember, his mom worked at his high school. She took nothing off fellow students., let alone teachers and administrators. She ran her little detention ward and he gladly avoided it like the proverbial plague for four long years. He went to class, played a little golf, maybe some basketball, and attended other big games and dances as teenage years demanded. But, he did yearn for bigger things to do.

Bigger things included contributing to the story of his school, which was told in the annual printing of the yearbook. He jumped in there. He and his pals, including his childhood friend, Kelly, and captured story and endless pictures about that high school experience. That went on for two or three years. He also served on and was eventually elected to lead the Key Club, a service organization sponsored by the local Kiwanis group. He led fundraisers for causes he cannot recall. But, they must have been worthy. He was nominated and elected to what was the Teen Board of his little town. Another service org that was a who's who of local kids. He remained just a who, so to speak. However, when it came to bell-ringing, he was the young man. He led that who's who crowd in wrist-dexterity, bell-ringing, and personality and raised the most cash from his little Kmart post during that Christmas Season. He has the Teen Board newsletter, somewhere in storage, to prove it. Your welcome, Salvation Army.

So, he certainly played in a lot of things…but, he was no player. He was an underachiever , One hit wonder with girls. Many dances. Many dates. Just one different girl every time. No repeats. All fun, but with a different girl every damn time. What was wrong with him? Was he too nice? Bad boys had wonderful girls. Is that what it takes? His dates were tall, short, blonde, brunette, smart, and on and on. One shot wonder he was and he just could not figure it out. There were three others that came after him. One just to piss off her boyfriend. Another, because their families got along well and they lived close to each other. And, one more who seemed to be really experienced in getting down and dirty, which scared the hell out of him. He ran. He ran very fast there. Remember, only Baptists lose their virginity to those they are married to….or will be really, really soon. It's a God thing.

Other horny guys partied with beautiful girls, smoked pot, drank beer, and just had a blast. He knew of such parties. He was never invited. It hurt, but it made sense. He did not smoke or drink.…yet. He was a 1980's freak. His "dare to be different" mantra began very early in life.

By the end of his social experiment of high school, he was leading a service org, represented his school at Boys State, elected to the National Honor Society, elected President of his senior class…and…drumroll, please…was elected Mr. BAC High School by his peers with none other than his love of 12 years, Miss BAC High School Beth. Yes, Beth from 1st grade. No joke. It really happened. Too bad that she only fell for football players and the like. His ship just had to sail on…

God knows what he's doing. He was just two cheerleaders away from his life-long, true Love.

He and his pals eventually graduated, thank God. He graduated ninth out of about 250 kids on the academic scale, with a 3.53 GPA, to be exact. Not Ivy League, for sure, but he did have a bit of fun and did not stress over it. Again, his parents' bar was so low that just getting into college was an achievement, let alone graduating.

Since he never made it to anywhere for Spring Break, his folks funded the Senior Trip with everyone to Myrtle Beach. It was a watershed week. He planned the entire trip for his dude friends and others followed. It was a first for him in a few ways. First time away from home with friends.

First time with that many girls alone. Almost first time with lots of booze. A swig of Jim Beam on a stopped ski lift at the age of 16 or 17 really doesn't really count.

Stuffing pure grain alcohol into a watermellon and eating it like its a buffet does count. He's sure that there was more than that…purchased by who???…but it was quite the fun week. Maybe, checking ID's back then was frowned upon.

The best story from that week was the one where the very hot girl comes to his room, crawls in his bed, and then a mutual friend shows up banging on his door and screaming for his night of potential pleasure to end. Classic. It was his first, live full-frontal nudity moment and one of the girls of his past shows up, scares the shit out of both of them, banging on the door and insisting to rescue her friend from his clutches. They scramble and she actually, no joke, hides in the cabinet under the bathroom sink. That crazy girl was welcomed in, failed find her friend, and then leaves in a huff. Then, his early, sexual opportunity leaves close behind her to make amends. They could have had so much fun. But, alas, they could have made a baby too. He wasn't properly prepared for such an encounter. It certainly worked out for the best.

The rest of that summer is not as memorable.

After another long summer, he escaped the BAC for another tiny town an hour north. They offered him a free ride to college…almost. His parents could not afford even the nominal cost of the local public university. But, in walked Miss Erica with her full scholarship to his destiny.

His academic and social work had earned him a full ride to college, sans housing. His mom and dad appreciated that and picked up the tab for his housing, in a fresh, new dorm that he and others broke in nicely. No air conditioning, but we had a nice box fan for the window. He and his two dorm-mates were just fine. He had never been camping, let alone lived with two other dudes. This was going to be interesting. One was an energetic guy who channeled that into cheerleading, which would eventually turn into a big business career for his roommate. The other was a cock-eyed, pimple-faced, overweight, and shifty former high-school quarterback that somehow wooed young girls in two different towns to be with him. He'll never figure that one out. Moving on...

He joined the Admissions Staff, selling the college to prospective students and their parents. He was elected to the Student Senate, where young people felt like they had some degree of power and ability to change things for the better. Not really.

Little did that boy know that only money and power, and money is power, really changes political institutions.

He was dropped off at college with the typical emotion and a few tears from mom. Dad could not be there. He was determined to leverage that full-tuition scholarship into something much bigger and better than what he knew back home. And, he did.

And, per usual, he was drawn to more cheerleaders. Damn his hormones! Damn him! And, God did.

HIs first one was much older. She flirted, but was not really interested. The second one had a stud, but nicest guy ever, boyfriend. That guy lived off campus with Roger, who made an inappropriate move on him after some homemade strawberry wine one night. That gay experience induced a little vomit. The third cheerleader was Asian-American. She was so hot, so experienced, and so intimidating. He freaked out again. His fourth did his laundry. His mom found that so funny. Four cheerleaders in his first semester. Pretty productive, but none were serious and none offered that flutter in the heart. Just a flutter below the heart that never consummated in any real experience. It was all on the surface.

Then, his roommate was busted. The former QB had kept up his girlfriend relationship back home while he kept another one going at college. He was a jerk. Everyone knew it. His girls did not. Then, all hell broke loose on him.

The betrayed girl at college was someone he knew. Through his first month or two of college, he was elected freshman Homecoming King with a cute blonde Queen he never knew. It was fine.

He was now in charge of the freshman Homecoming committee and enjoyed planning their part of the fall celebration. Most of all, his future girlfriend and wife was on that committee. She was a cheerleader, of course. She had been dropped while cheering and busted her tailbone. She had her ass kicked by a jerk QB and a fellow cheerleader too. She was damaged goods, but brilliant. She had earned a full-tuition, just like him.

He liked her. He felt sorry for her. He was young.

So was she. They fell in love, after his QB roommate's cover was blown. Remember, there were no mobile phones. No internet. No email. No ability to quickly transfer information. DOS programming was the standard. Technology was useless to communicate anywhere. Pumping coins into a pay phone was the way to get to others fast. There was no easy way to bust a cheater. Just good ole word-of-mouth was it. And, that it did. In just a few months, stud boy QB had been outed and the rest is history.

That second semester is a blur, except for a couple of things.

He never knew un-closeted gay guys until college. Roger was his first. An older queen trying to take advantage of a newbie drunk. Next, a pack of gay guys who were very nice and chose to live a town away together while attending college.

Well, one of them found himself on the viaduct (old bridge connecting the campus) getting the shit kicked out of him by some fine, upstanding, Baptist, bible-thumpin boys. He was a bit scarred by that and cannot forget it. What was the mandatory attendance to chapel for a sermon every week all about? Where was the moral fiber? Where was common, secular decency? Not there, on that bridge, it seemed.

Gay bashing evidently eluded the window of sin and "Do unto others..." part of the Bible. Quite the lesson, as they trudged into mandatory worship every Monday, Wednesday, or Friday.

Also, he had a good friend named Mike, who was thrown under the local jail by the FBI for producing fake ID's. Who knew? He did not . But, what a lesson about violating federal law, in that tiny town.

Back to his new love. They were engaged and married in just about 18 months. Go figure. They knew what they wanted...or thought so. They dated that second semester of their freshman year. They hung out with great friends on and off campus. They each excelled at studies and kept their respective full scholarships. They may or may not have been some golden couple that freshman year, but it was a great time for them.

After one long summer of burning up the phone lines (sorry for the AT&T bill, mom & dad), they returned to college as Resident Assistants, which earned each free room and board. Thus, both were now attending college with no expense for them and their parents...except for fun money, of course.

That fun money did fund a new fondness for liquor, which others had to procure from an hour away, since his college was in a dry county. Not a problem, just a pain. To this day, he cannot enjoy a screwdriver without thinking about his early college days.

Buckle up, buttercup. They had it made. Both had great dorms, a little responsibility, and were on their own away from their hometowns. Not wild ones, but fun loving kids trying to figure out their 19th and 20th years on the planet.

He liked vodka. She like nothing like that and abided by all campus rules. They were different. But, they had never been in love like this. He tried to smoke Marlboro's and Swisher Sweet "cigars" and she did not . She was truly Baptist and he was running from all that forced religion thing. Maybe , those were very big signs of things to come.

Each soldiered on that sophomore year, until they could not. For whatever reason, she could not handle the "small town thing" where "everyone knows everything" about you. She grew to not accept the small college life and she decided to leave halfway through that sophomore year, full scholarship be damned.

Not that they had anything to hide…except one little thing. They did escape to a seedy motel one time, somewhere between college and his hometown. And, somehow, they checked in and had a rather erotic night together, which could never happen on campus without a lot of off-campus help. They were private and this first experience for both was kept private, as far as they knew. In less than a year, their real consummation would be very real and a honeymoon would follow…at the age of 19.

After she left college, he went on with a nice apartment off-campus…yes, he gave up his RA position too…and that lasted one month. Sorry, landlord. He could not handle being apart. He left his college too. He lost it too. Neither had ever been in love like that. They burned up the phone lines again and also the interstate, as money allowed.

They were engaged and, sadly, he cannot recall how or when that happened. That's just pretty darn sad.
A recent study showed that the average male admits to 14 or more partners over their lifetime. If that's so, he's 12 short.

He eventually made love to two women and both were married to him or really close to being so. Just two. No more. Two for a lifetime….he's just that weird and he's fine with that.

One way or another, he and his first love stayed connected over those tough months. Again, no internet. No Skype. No easy way to connect except expensive phone calls, which were indulged by both sets of parents. Eventually, not sure how, there was a ring and they were married in her hometown. Lots of coral blue accented tuxedos and dresses. It was 1980's beautiful.

His dad was his best man and that was fitting. There was no other best man, so to speak. He was the only one, as weird as that may have been. His dad made a dashing best man, actually. His mom was lovely too. A simple wedding and a simple reception. A simple life to begin, but they needed to finish those college degrees. No slackers allowed here.

A quick honeymoon on the Atlantic and then reality kicks in. They had researched, at the library, various colleges and universities and have somehow found their fit.

She wanted Interior design and he wanted Marketing & Entrepreneurship majors. They found it in a dull little town in Indiana. They moved into married housing. No jobs. Student loans covered expenses that their scholarships and RA stipends used to cover. But, they were determined teens.

She enrolled in the local university and he went looking for a job to pay the bills. Their parents helped, of course, but he needed to find a job that would allow them to move on as adults. After a few months, he was desperate and went to a loan-shark like firm called Snelling & Snelling. His folks helped him out, yet again, and gave him the $1,400 for a $14,000 per year job. Quite the finders fee. It was his first retail job was at Color Tile. Home improvement store before big boxes took over that market. He had that above salary, but the cake was made in the form of spiffs (commission) on various products. It paid the bills, as they say.

Always looking, as she went to school, he found what he thought would be even better in the "finance" industry. More like legalized loan-sharking. USA Financial sounded so legit. But, it was the first of several nauseating business experiences. He was the Assistant Manager, which was really the bill collector for the business. Imagine a tiny office where all of the staff are in one room and his full-time job was rifling through a box of paper cards and calling as many as possible who missed their payment date. A business that legally charged upwards of 26% interest per annum, if memory serves. Seemed criminal, but he needed the job. It wasn't his first ethical and moral dilemma over his career. But, this business was legal and his job was one of necessity.

Basically, he called the same people every month, unless they started paying without a prompt, and he created a rapport with some of those who could not pay their bills. Getting folks to drop by and pay or to have payments arrive by mail was the honey to his manager's vinegar. His boss seemed to enjoy screaming and demeaning staff and customers alike. He was quite the jerk of a manager. A valuable lesson for this young fellow. His boss would even take the phone from him to scream at a customer and threaten them in ways that may have not been allowed by law. That was his way. The experience made the Color Tile job look pretty good…but, he didn't have to work weekends at USA. He quickly grew to loathe that manager, even if that job paid the bills. As his young wife entered her last year of college, he made another change and planned for his return to school to finish his degree. Thank God. He found his third job on campus and it fit him better than anything since mowing lawns as a kid. And, no working on weekends again! He joined the university newspaper in the sales department. Selling ads for the paper fit him perfectly. He called on local entrepreneurs and pitched each the investment and potential ROI by advertising in the university newspaper.

He would then be able to enroll in school and get that B.S. degree, which is funny. B.S. would be a big part of his future business career.

In that last year of college, he was able to take 60 credit hours of classes in just one calendar year. students take, but he needed to catch up. Twice what most

He had taken two years off from college and he caught up in just a year, with three summer sessions. No summer travel for those two that year.

He also lost his Papaw during that time. His granddad, barber, and another religious role-model. His Papaw even told customers and friends that his grandson made straight A's and was going to be a preacher too someday. Neither was true, but his Papaw thought so. He never corrected him. His Papaw just passed in his sleep around 70 years of age. In a weird twist, he had a dream the night he died about his Papaw and he got the call the next morning. No more conversations on the front porch swing, for sure.

Graduation came with little fanfare and no celebration. He just wanted out of there. He married too young, almost lost it towards the end, left his wife briefly and returned home, but finally got it together and they moved back to her hometown to live with her parents. They were great. Very nice to care for them as they searched for work.

His university professors had bragged for years about how the corporate recruiting, especially the pharmaceutical industry, would storm the campus and pluck up every business student like ripe fruit. Lucrative jobs for their graduates was the norm and he and his peers should be prepared. Sadly, they never came. A new recession arrived right on-time. They both hit the road with newly minted degrees and several thousand dollars in college debt.

Recession be damned.

She found a little interior design thing to do. He found his next opportunity with B2B phone system sales. Back then, every business needed a phone system and voice mail connectivity and the business owner may be the only one with that huge, mobile bag phone…it was quite ridiculous. A huge bag phone you toted around like luggage. He became the sales and service conduit between business owners and manager, their staff, and the techs who installed the products he sold. This was a little place to experience real-world entrepreneurs from both sides of the negotiating table. His education was always continuing. A first of many small, family business experiences to come. Sell, sell, sell. That's what he did.

Then, here came another jerk. One small, Irish jerk. Somehow, he and his newest jerk boss crossed paths and the jerk made him an offer that he could not refuse.

He just became a dad. His first girl was born and they moved to a cool condo in an old, former school with a cool pool and life was good. Too cats, Megan and Muffy, too.

He was young. He did not stay a cat person for long. However, he's a dad now and that's forever. His new job was as a VP of Sales in a small distributorship of new coin laundry equipment. His jerk boss did teach him a lot about sales, but also a lot about how to not be a business owner, husband, and father. He would stab anyone in the back for cash. It was quite the continuing education. Of course, after building a dozen or so new businesses for coin laundry entrepreneurs , he decided that he had taken enough and started his own company to consult and advise those wanting to get into that business. His intent was to be the middle-man, not a distributor of equipment, and advise clients about the pro's and con's of each coin laundry brand. He has business cards made. He had a letterhead created. He had it all figured out, or so he thought. He had just raked in $75,000 that last year, with great success at just 25 years of age. Back then, that was a lot. They even bought a new home in a brand new neighborhood…perfect. What could go wrong?

His second, perfect daughter was born about then and the family of four was set up nicely…until…the wheels fell off. His new business was challenged by the jerk. The same jerk that motivated him to jump ship when the jerk demanded that he locate a new business too close to another business they created for another owner in that same city. His urban territories were maxed out, in his opinion.

Not so, said the jerk, who wanted to cram more investors on top of one another and he did not agree with said jerk. He convinced 3 investors to join him and to keep their business plans and purchases moving forward. Simple enough. Cut those consulting deals and keep moving forward with the jerk, as contractually demanded, and then invest his fees back into a new flower shop that tied in nicely to his wife's interior design career. So simple. Such a business was available in their small hometown, with a built in customer base and cash flow. Bonus, a funeral home was just 100yards away too. They need flowers almost daily.

All could have been fine, but it was not. The jerk threatened and eventually sued him for taking off on his own with 3 clients who chose to go with him. At the same time, the stresses of two little girls, his business decisions, and whatever other issues led them to a getaway to Florida to reconnect and figure out where they were headed. them, so they could figure this out. Their girls aunt joined

They did not. A few months later, she advised him that she wanted out. They discussed, argued, cried, etc. over three days. After the third day, he gave up and spent the next three weeks keeping up the air of normalcy while training her in the art of running a business, the flower shop.

They slept in the same bed for three weeks, since he refused to be kicked out of the bed he bought….and it was his last victory for a while. He was the loser. Two girls lost. She lost something too. Everyone lost…for a while. Both bottoms had fallen out of his personal and professional life. Even the Baptist church, where he was elected one of the youngest deacons ever, turned on him and left nasty notes on his car that last Sunday morning. WWJD?

Of course, another note, a love letter, was found later that offered insight into the grass-must-be-greener thoughts of his soon to be ex-wife and mother of his children.

He said his goodbyes to his girls, who could not understand at the ages of 2 and 9 months. He drove home and found his dad at the garage door, somewhat in shock. He told him what happened and, for the second time ever, they both cried together. It was another sad thing. Marriage lasts through anything, but not these GenX'ers. After spending a little time with his parents, he took off again. He bolted for Colorado, a place he fell in love with on their family trip there years before. Summitt County, CO to be exact. With the help of caffeine pills, he made it there in about 21 hours, driving his sporty Ford Probe. Yes, a Probe. Insert joke here.

He had $1,000 in his pocket and he intended to blow it. He arrived in Breckenridge, pulled into the parking lot of a condo complex, realized that this was not his answer, slumped over in tears, and then promptly hit I-40 again and returned home. Lots of miles and tears later, he pulled over in Amarillo, TX. Exhausted and needing a break from the road, he found his first "gentleman's club". It was neither a club, nor filled with gentlemen. Lesson learned there. He struck out again. Could he do anything right? His marriage was a bust. His traditional fatherhood was a bust. His trip was a bust. His attempt to escape was a bust. He was one big bust who found himself on the shoulder of I-40 East in downtown Little Rock, AR, crying his eyes out and watching for the best time to jump in front of any given semi-truck that would surely end his pain. He measured the timing and velocity of each tractor trailer that whizzed by at really high speeds. One quick dash and it's over. His life. His parents life would suffer. And, his young girls could not be the same either. All of that rushed into his brain. His quick relief would certainly leave decades of mystery and unknowns for the last few he loved deeply. God stopped him. Or he did…or both, and not for the last time.

He made it home to his parents home and took over his old bedroom at the age of 25. A grown man starting over with two little girls to love, enjoy, and support. It took a good six months to finalize details, but his family helped him fund the support needed until he found his next sales opportunity that fall.

When not burning up the interstate to be with his girls every other weekend, he searched for work back home. Not a desk job. Another sales or marketing opportunity that offered a different challenge each day was his objective. He found an industrial tool sales opportunity in his hometown. He sold a dozen or so of the most unusual and useful tools and gadgets that any mechanic could appreciate. But, to say that he was a fish out of water would by a huge understatement. He lasted three months and he moved on and backwards to business phone sales again. He knew that he would hate it and he did, but it beat selling tools. He would be selling to business owners and managers again. His new company was based in Nashville and he had to go there to train for his new sales opportunity. And, his new boss was gay. A nice guy. No jerk this time. It was another first for him. A nice, gay boss and antique shop owner from Belle Meade. All things considered, the business should be financially sound, he thought.

A week's worth of sales training and self-loathing passed and he was on his way home. Then, with his new cell phone or carrier pigeon , he cannot recall, word arrived that there was a Gator Bowl party on the west side of town and would time out with his return from training that night.
12/30/1994

That night changed his life, his girls' lives, their parents lives, and his yet-to-be born boys' lives….forever.
God really knew what he was doing.

His cousin extended a, invitation to this football party and a home where he knew no one but his cousin. He somehow accepted and went with the hope that his spirits could be lifted.

And, there she was. The Love of his life. He just did not know it yet. That took few days more.

She was sitting in the living room floor, arms flailing around, and telling a story or two. Who is that, he asked himself. She was the only single or unattached gal there. He was the only underemployed, divorced, and depressed guy there. She was the greatest medicine for his condition that he ever received. She had an aura and spirit that, fortunately, could not be tempered. Their true love story began that night and hasn't stopped over two decades later.

Coincidentally, his new Love had been with her exboyfriend for about the same six years that he was married to his former love. Long story there that she should tell someday. She was single and not looking for love then. He was single, depressed, and just looking for fun again. Anywhere.

Anyone. But it was her. For months now, women were just evil and marriage would never be an option again. Too painful. In just one evening, he was welcomed by complete strangers, thanks to his cousin, entertained by an odd mix of characters, and then met and barely got to know the future Love of his life. Of course, always the realist, he whipped out his wallet full of pictures and showed her his little girls, just in case this was a deal-killer for her. He could not handle any more rejection. His logic told him "If she's going to bolt, let's get it over with now". She did not run. She met his challenge with interest, questions, and conviviality. It was one great night. He doesn't even recall who won the game. His life was about to change for the better and he prayed for just that.

When the night was ending, she invited him to her apartment with that bunch and others, 20-30 young people, for their New Year's party the following night. Great food and drink? His new Love? Dick Clark's ball dropping? He's in. And, that tiny sliver of pride he had remaining seemed to grow just a bit. He was smitten in, just one night. Night two clinched the deal. They were both smitten in just about 24 hours, if the kiss at midnight was any indication. He yelled across that tiny living room for his Love to come over and they locked lips to the ball dropping in Times Square. Their first kiss and it was a big one. Hello, 1995! That magical winter just kept on going. She had a woodburning fireplace in that little apartment and, boy, did they ever use it. He chopped and reloaded wood as often as he could . They both had sales careers now and worked their schedules around gathering back at her apartment. Work was necessary, but totally in the way of curling up on her couch. No sleepovers. Just great times getting to know each other. Those afternoons divulging everything to one another were priceless. All cards were on the proverbial table.

In a matter of weeks, they were ready to be engaged. They were the only ones ready for that. Her friends were skeptics. Their parents were too, not that it really mattered. He wrote a heart-felt letter (yes, pen and paper letter) to her parents about his Love and his love for her that seemed to turn those skeptics into converts. His parents just knew that he would do whatever he was determined to do, just as he did at age 19 with his first love. Their biggest test was her meeting his two, little girls. He had been spending all of his legally allowed time with them solo for about 9 months. That dynamic was about to change. By then, just shy of 15mos & 3yrs old, respectively, here's a new person he would like them to meet. That weekend arrived.

Both girls stuck to each other or dad like glue. His new Love had a rough weekend. His girls did not understand and did not welcome her without putting up a wall. However, by the end of that weekend, they turned, hugged her, and showed a little love for the first time right before he and his Love pulled out of their great-grandparents driveway. Little victories.

Somewhere in that new year, he gets a call from his former sister-in-law and their family is panicked about his girls and ex-wife moving to Iowa. Yep, turned out, and he has the love letter, that an old high-school flame had been corresponding with her and convinced her of a better life up in Iowa, while they were married. She took the bait. But, he legally yanked the hook out of her mouth. Legally, she could not move their girls more than 100 miles away without permission from him. His former family asked for his help and he delivered. Not for them, but for those two girls. A first of a few battles to come. You're welcome, former family.

The antique, circa 1930's, engagement band and wedding ring were bought and they made it official on the front steps of their downtown church. Dinner overlooking the old Worlds Fair Park was also part of that night.

He would elope, if she would. But, alas, this is her day. The day that girls dream about. And, it's time to party like it's 1995, because it was. Plans started immediately and she juggle her sales career with a wedding and he just wanted to fast forward to the honeymoon. But where?

Myrtle Beach again? Never. How about somewhere awesome, but affordable? Little did they know where they were headed.

Their wedding was a classic, pre-social media event with real photographers, video taping, and living in the moment there at their church and, afterwards, at the Museum of Art two blocks away. The wedding was quick, but the walk across the street with those two little girls is still embedded in their minds.

Just as the walk to the girls grandparents' car during the reception. One tearful goodbye after dancing with two princesses in their arms in the great hall of their Museum of Art. That was a sweet time dancing and enjoying friends and family. And the Museum was a perfect setting for hours of fun, food, music, and dancing.

With their girls gone, it was time to start thinking "aloha". Yes, the received lots of great gifts and cash, but the best had to be what her long-time friend gave them…Delta miles to go to Maui. They could have never afforded that airfare. Thank God for Kim. She made their honeymoon as classic as the wedding. After spending their wedding night at the airport Hilton, they flew to Maui and they were more than a little giddy. They needed this. It was magical.
He had researched for months, in that pre-Google, oldschool way, and found a B&B on Maui that was a nice, hillside home with a small room for rent…$59 a night. Sweet. And a full breakfast was included. They had about $1,000 budgeted for the entire week. Half for the room and half for food, fun, and souvenirs. Cheapest Maui honeymoon ever, they thought.

Maui is a tourist paradise for many reasons. And, they were happy to be there. The flight took all day and they could care a less. They arrived, picked up their convertible, threw the top down, and headed straight to Momma's Fish House in Piai.

A little town on the north coast, right before you get on the road to Hana. That would be later. Mama's is iconic. They had their pictures taken and the tiki torches lined up perfectly with each of their heads like fire was shooting out of each newlywed head at sunset. He must find that picture and all of those many pictures they took on real film with a real camera. He pretty sure that they had no mobile phone at that time…not even a flip phone yet. Mama's really delivered that night!

Their first adventure, so to speak. Their first adventure together and they were in the presence of tourists & adventurers each never knew. And, as for sailing the world…little did they know back then that they would do that, as well. It begins.

They had a fantastic meal at Mama's that first night in Maui. Blew 20% of their meal budget in just one night, even splitting an entree'.

Appetizers and a bottle of wine might have helped a bit. Lesson learned.

No matter. They checked into their B&B and that family was so nice. The put on quite the breakfast spread every morning. But, FYI, one can overdose on fresh fruit of mangoes, papaya, guava, and pineapple. Trust him.

Greatest laxative ever. Fair warning. Once thoroughly cleaned out, they hit the road for fun and sun each day.

In August, there doesn't seem to be a bad day in Maui. A convertible greatly enhances one's experience, but you could be on foot, bike, or surry, for crying out loud. That island is that perfect mix of open spaces and touristy shopping and eating. He and his Love found their special spots all over that island. From the beach to the town of Lahaina to the top of the volcano to the local winery to all of the lovely spots on and around the road to Hana….all moments were beautiful and very special. Life was very, very good that week!

They had no plans. Just a Foder's guidebook, free airfare, and a cheap B&B to rest. This island was there's to explore and kick off their married life together. Sweet.

They even met another young couple and took them in their convertible up to the Haleacula volcano sunset above the clouds, which was amazing.

They took very tasty fruit, brie cheese plates, and wine too. It was a fun drive up and a great time with new friends on top of the island peak.

The cruise home was chilly with the top down, even in August. The top came up and the leftover food found its way into the cubby where the top settles when down. The next morning, he and his love loaded up for the beach and there was an unreal smell in that car. Oh, dear God, the smell. It took a while, but they found the leftover brie in that cubby and quickly aired out their ride for the day.

Their adventure continued for the rest of that week. They drove the entire island, including the famous road to Hana with hundreds of turns and switch-backs and a rough trail past Hana that you can brave to come full circle back to civilization. Should of had a Jeep, but the Pontiac convertible was all they could afford. They enjoyed the road and the town of Hana and also be big bumps and grinds along the dirt trail back to Kihei and back up to Lahaina.

Somehow, in the touristy course of events, this new married couple found themselves offered a condo tour in exchange for a free Luau experience at the beachfront Marriott resort. They could not afford to stay there, but to enjoy and feast and a show and other tourists for free? Yes, please.

They book the tour, which lasted 90 minutes, and it was cool. It also timed out with the first and only rain shower they had all week. But, they were inside and licking their chops about the luau to come. Of course, they could not afford the condo timeshare or any condo there. But, they fit the demographic the wanted and they gladly took the deal. They enjoyed a sunny morning, peeled away for the tour as a shower rolled in, and hit the sunny beach afterwards. It was just meant to be.

They eventually went to their booked Luau on the west coast of Maui, in Kaanapali. It was a beautiful sunset Luau with a couple of hundred folks at huge, long tables and with a big stage for the dancing and other entertainment. Great food and endless Mai-Tai's were enjoyed all evening, as their only fancy night moved on. By the time the luau MC took the mic, they were feeling fine. The MC asked for the crowed applaud the first lady of the Philippines, who was in attendance. And, they did. He then asked for the nationality or where others there were from. After a bunch of responses, and after they had discussed with their table just where they were from…he springs up from his chair and yells "Australia!!! Guday ! Guday!!!", waving his drink in the air, much to the surprise of his Love and the entire table.

The applause was outstanding. He sat back down and the table's silence was ended by a lot of laughs. That was a really fun night.

Fresh fruit, great meals, a nice pool, sunny beaches, and a decent convertible…and lots of libations and great experience…their perfect honeymoon really happened. One great start to the a great, loving relationship that began a little over 20 years ago, as this is written. Almost 27 years down and decades more to come. Here they go.

A new marriage. A new apartment. And, a new job for him. That's what they flew home to… a new life for both.

He applied for a GM position at a small media firm months before and came in 2nd to a former pharma rep who somehow got that job. But, his persistence worked and the monthly hand-written notes (email wasn't a thing then) phone calls, and voice mails to the owner paid off. He was made an offer and was hired by the GM to market the media business the week before his wedding. It was the beginning of quite the 13 year roller-coaster ride.

His new job was pretty simple. Call up radio stations all across America and Canada and sell each on taking your firm's money. He was in the radio media buying business. Block time, not :60 or :90 spots.

24-26 minute blocks were his targets. Sure, most stations balked, due to their programming and their other options to keep their holy station pure. But, he could be convincing. Their little media company went from 175 stations, when he arrived, to 425 in just 17 months. It was good growth and everyone noticed. Moreover, profitability grew even more. There was lots of cash to go around from stations to staff to the the call center up in Maine.

But, how did they do it, you may ask? It was simple, but brilliant. Find good to great products that are slow to sell, by their owners. Build a great "live" talk show around each. Take the customer calls and sell, sell, sell.

It wasn't easy. If the sales guys were led by a station GM who came up as a programmer, tough sale. If the GM, came into his position as a sales guy, much better sales opportunity. Remember, he was selling station reps on taking his firm's money. Should be easy, but it was not. He made it work for everyone, including his own family.

In just 17 months, the GM's stories and lies caught up. He was ready to take over for that lame GM. Months earlier, the owner had asked, sitting in his living room upstairs (yes, his media firm took up his entire basement, which was really cool. A fireplace and tv and little offices built in. Nice), "what is you goal?".

He simply replied "to run your company when you want to move on to something else." The owner laughed. He did not. He was 28 years of age and fully capable to take on the challenge with a small staff he liked and trusted.

He took over, after more than tripling the revenue and profitability of that little, homegrown media company. But, as with any business, greed dictated change. Either from existing partners, lawsuits, or just internal greed, every single business will be challenged, see terrible declines, and/or face big changes to survive.

Their challenge was to seek autonomy from a talented partner who seemed to grow too big for his britches. He and his team booked the infomercial media and the partner in Maine took the calls per show, growing from just a few sales reps to a staff of over 1,000. The writing was on the proverbial wall. Why don't they book their own media and produce their own shows and not split the profits? It was coming.

Thus, his firm's owner decided to step out, produce shows as usual, but then send the calls to another place. Another partner, JB, stepped up and hooked the media firm up with a call center north of Sacramento, CA. It was a great fit and it lasted over ten years.

Their products included hair-growth formulas, a capsaicin pain-reliever, a pre-Viagra natural "boing" product, a fat-absorbing pill that soaked up pounds to be pooped out, and a natural hormone releaser that made people feel younger. All-natural solutions that their owners could not quite make work in the marketplace. Many other products were pitched, but only a few succeeded and went on to sell tens of millions of dollars per year.

Put an almost half-hour show together with a killer host, edit the show

well, add all of the bumper music and sales spots, and you have
something.

Most of all, his highs and lows of going into the sales and management
roles were dwarfed by his freedom to break away on Friday and go get
his girls or stay somewhere with them and his Love. The wicked desk job
and daily phone work was all worth it, but he would never go back to
such an existence. He and his Love absolutely wore out the interstate
system every other weekend, either bringing their two little girls home or
staying with them in decent motels or sweet B&B's in little towns. It was
only 4-5 days a month. They made the most of it. It was all they had.
Every other Sunday was one sad drive home, just as every other Friday
was a joy. You just had to be there.

As for these two lovebirds, every other DINK (duel income, no kids)
weekend was fulfilling too. They had a great apartment with two pools,
one adult-only, another family, and it was a fun crowd. It was also close
to downtown, where they had dated and where they went to church. It
was a great first year together. His Love's career was chugging along.
His was just getting started with a fun group that was making really
good money. But, he had to get out of this town and explore, preferably
with his Love. He searched for career development or professional
courses that could help the firm, but would allow him to travel and get
the hell out of his town for free. NYC was calling. He found a Direct
Marketing and the Law conference in the spring of that year. This first
of a few conferences was being held in mid-town Manhattan. That is
where another love affair began. He flew up, at company expense, and he
was really there. This bumpkin from the BAC really made it to the big
city. Yankees were looked down upon back home. He did not care. He
loved the city, the vibe, the smells, and the attitudes.

He flew into Laguardia for the first time and hopped into a nice Lincoln
for the ride into town. For the first time ever, he was in a real,
metropolitan capital. And, he knew it. Fortunately, after all of the
conference stuff, his Love would arrive soon and share in this experience.
That week, they fell in love with the City together. The Park. The food.
The theatre.

What else did they need? Okay, his company AMEX came in really handy too for the flight, great meals, and, then, his boss and owner of the firm insisted that they go see a Broadway show. "You're in New York. Go see a show on the company. Have fun!" his boss insisted. Nice.

How fitting the choice was…"How to Succeed in Business Without Really Trying" was his choice. Matthew Broderick in the lead role and if he could only be sent back 30+ years, this could be him selling widgets… well, never mind. It was him in theory. That was an amazing introduction to Broadway and his new-found love of live theatre. And, I mean LOVE. Throw in his real Love, a few drinks, and meals at Sardi's and this was a new experience that could not be beat. Speaking of beat, back up to his first night there.

He thought he could handle the subway. He could not. He jumped off his plane, checked into the Marriott, and jumped right on the train to the Bronx for a Yankees game. The train took him north and kept going. He freaked out. He did not ask anyone for help. His train passed the Bronx. And he took some other exit and crossed under the tracks to jump back on and head back to his cozy hotel.

He just wasn't ready for the subway connection and Bronx thing yet . You just had to be there.

Back to the show! It was amazing! That first taste of Broadway was epic for both of them. Both had experienced theatre, but not quite like this. They were hooked and their kids would be too very soon. They planned to get their girls up there ASAP. And, they did. NYC plays a huge part in their history and in their dreams to this day. Central Park is remarkable. He helped start a non-profit org in his hometown that could secure thousands of acres of park space for fun and relaxation. Not a Central Park, but a huge, connected space for walking, running, biking, hiking, napping, and general fun times in a uberconservative neck of the woods….almost all privately funded. Unheard of? Yes…around this neck of the midsouth. There was also the food…oh, the food. Lots of places, but 7th ave seem to have the Greek solution @ Molyvos and the other thing @ The Red Eye Grill and stop everything for lunch @ the Carnegie Deli. All good. Sardi's before or after theatre too. As if it

couldn't get any better…there was Johnnies. They just stumbled upon it.
A shotgun, old, Italian destination a few feet off of Times Square. So
cool…so stuck in time. And, they walked in and there he was. Anthony.
Anthony Canterella. The man. Picture silver hair slicked back, blue
shirt, French cuffs, and an Italian attitude that could never be contained.

He was and is the best. That "little It'ly" accent was magic. He knew
made men. He knew secrets. He was a joy to chat with at the bar, which
he did prior to his Love's arrival…that's how he knew where to g0 with
her! They just connected. They also shared that glass and mirrored spot
with their girls in the coming years, not that they would remember…but
he never will. Lots of mirrors, crystal chandeliers , Rat Pack tunes, and
simple, delicious food and drink in that shotgun space. Johnnie would
have been proud all of those years later. Anthony still lives in Queens
with his wife, who he met during their traveling years. He called her
"rice", since she was from the south and called in an order for cooked
rice one day. Needless to say, Anthony had fun with that order and has
joked about it ever since. A Yankee and a southern belle made good, it
seems.
They each had the travel bug and they liked it.

Just a few decades ahead of travel and fun…love. First, Maui, then
Hilton Head, then NYC. Next, annual beach trips. One such trip is just
enough for a while. It's all they could afford. Two, young marrieds with
two beautiful girls that they only legally had for a few days a months, a
few weeks in the summer, and over Father's Day weekend (for a while),
Thanksgiving weekend, and the afterChristmas party too. Dads gotta do
what you gotta legally can do, it seems, when you only have visitation
rights.

It was one of the last summer weeks that he and she would be limited, by
employer's restraints, to just one week of fun with their kids in the
summer.

That first was taking the girls to L.A. The L.A. The place where dreams
come true. Sand. Salt. And great fried shrimp. Lower Alabama was the
place to reunion. A family reunion was an annual thing, but most there
lived within a few hours or just less than an hour away. He and his Love

lived almost 10 hours away.

Stars & Bars flag hanging off the deck was fine, right next to the Auburn flag. They were, and are, the family to party with whenever invited. The "kids" were on their own and still behaved like those who just wanted to keep the fun going. Self-sufficiency is a very good thing. That Aframe home was and is the Alabama gathering place for decades. Kids growing up there. Adult kids growing up there. New kids marrying in and divorcing around there. Some older ones dying out and not being there. That one home can tell the tale of a big family and many life changes. But, they always end up there again, just as they will do this summer and for, hopefully, many to come.

Past their honeymoon, a few great trips, and heading home to sweet home Alabama, travel became their way to experience life beyond their small part of the world in the BAC.

On another "business trip", they enjoyed Laguna Beach, CA like no other beach. The water was too damn cold, but it did not matter. Everyone was beautiful. Too beautiful.
"Baywatch".
Even police officers were actors let go from

Laguna was and is a remarkable artist colony by the Pacific Ocean, not to mention great foodie options too. Then came more of Hilton Head, Scottsdale, AZ, and then on to Puerto Rico, Negril, Jamaica, the amazing Turks & Caicos…and the USVI/BVI's. They did them all together and a few with their kids.

The timing escapes him, but no matter. They were all amazing and offer lots of relaxation, great times, and fun for all of their ages.

That last one, the USVI/BVI's, were huge. That was where he fell in love with the Caribbean Sea….their future home…much future, but whatever.

They sailed on a killer monohull, were introduced to catamarans, and other multihull boats and yachts. Yes, yachts that he could not come close to valuing.

His business partner made sure of that. That guy knew what he knew, more ways than one.

Very soon after he took over the firm and became it's GM and Managing Partner, he and his Love went on a winter vacation to that magical place of the Virgin Islands. Not that he needed another love. He just needed to go where he and his Love had never been before…and, they did.

All three partners and their much better halves flew down to Miami for an overnight, before heading to the greatest getaway ever, since Maui. Over dinner, in a cool place overlooking Miami, the subject of passports came up. Why? They were flying to St. Thomas tomorrow. It's a United States' territory. However, if they wanted to go to Tortola and other BVI territories…well…you know. It's a post-9/11 world now and we know what is expected. Back then, not so much.

It was a problem, but not one that two resourceful moms could not fix. Both of his and his Love's moms found their respective birth certificates, which were good for authorities back then, and the FedEx man on a dinghy arrived soon after they were on that 75' sailboat and delivered their credentials. That was the last time they travelled out of the upper 50 states without a passport.

Funny thing. The Cuban cigars smoked just fine. That week flew by and way too fast. Time flies on such a huge sailboat with a crew of 3. A 20-something Captain, huge sailboat with a crew of 3. A 20-something Captain, something chef took great care of them. Yeah, life was very, very good that week and was one that none of them would ever forget. Many years later, that lovely sail and anchorages would take on a far greater meaning.

Hundreds of pictures, conversations, dreams, swims, and sails later, the group of 6 friends would never repeat such a trip. It was a one-time life experience, like most, and one they would never forget…and would take on a far deeper meaning too years later, when one couple tragically leaves them and earth for good.

Back at home, they lived the high life, as well, in a small house in a sweet neighborhood. Not a bad place at all to return from paradise.

The young couple rented for their first year and enjoyed that place in a big way…two pools! But, they needed their own space and a fun community with it. They found it in a lovely, old neighborhood.

It was meant to be.

A modest home with lots of potential it was in the perfect neighborhood for them. Nothing but young couples, widows, and older gay couples, who had the best gardens and manicured lawns. Gay seemed to equate to higher property values. Who could argue with that?

Their home had lots of light and light hardwood floors upstairs, a huge, private patio out back surrounded by ivy & tall trees, and a man's man, dark basement with wood paneling and fresh new carpet. All dark down there, with a killer stone hearth and a new wood stove. His in-laws gave them $5k to buy the home and threw in a bonus, the Jotel wood stove that could heat the home all winter, if they chose to go rustic. They didn't need it, but, oh, did they use it as a fireplace and a heat source. He loved and loves the smell of burning hardwood…not to mention the romance of it all in his man cave. Their young girls loved that basement too. Lots of cozy space for sleepovers and family time down there.

Soon after moving in, he and his Love became parents of a new kind. Dog lovers will understand. His name was Snickers or Butterscotch, depending on who you asked. It didn't matter. He was the cutest puppy ever and his home next door was not for him. All of his siblings had died in the mountains, when that family camped there.

He was the last one left and he seemed to need attention from his neighbors. They fed him. They loved on him. Eventually, he approached his twitchy neighbor and just flat out asked if they could keep the puppy. His neighbor agreed and they named him Bud. He was a handsome redbone hound & beagle mix puppy.

That was the beginning of a 14-year love. Bud was his first dog, at the age of 27. Their first dog to love together. However, they did have, as evidenced on their furniture, a bit of a glandular problem. The back-door kind. The nasty, leave smelly deposits behind kind. Anal-gland issues sound funny, but the smell and spots are anything but that. Thus, after a trip to the vet and hearing all that was involved with freeing Bud of this (no good options here), he resolved to relieve Bud of is doggy hemorrhoids every 2-3 days for over 14 years. Yes, except for vacations and Bud staying at his kennel, he grabbed his tail with his left hand, like a handle, and squeezed Bud's butt glands, like marbles full of ick, and emptied each efficiently and effectively without a frequent trips to the vet.

Just a technique that his Love never quite mastered and she was fine with that. Bud was quite relieved too, every few days when he grew more and more uncomfortable. Bud's vet was quite impressed, as well.

Not only at the chore he took on, but the decision to not risk his beloved dog's existence after a risky surgery. Funny what you will do for a dog you really love.

Speaking of true loves, their girls were growing up too, in love with their new mom and ready to see the world past the beach trips. Those two cuties were introduced to Laguna Beach, CA, Scottsdale, AZ, Washington DC, Turks & Caicos, and, of course, Midtown Manhattan, NYC. All great places from coast to coast. Beach towns, artist colonies, desert towns, historic places, the Caribbean, and, of course, Broadway and Central Park. Their first Broadway show as a family was "The Sound of Music", on the front row. Same row for "Annie get Your Gun" and Bernadette Peters winked at them as she shot at them with her fingers. Big moment there. There was also "The Lion King". Not his favorite, but the girls liked it.

There were others shows that he cannot recall, but the Playbill collection in storage should jog his memory someday.

Central Park by day and Broadway by night and the Carnegie Deli in-between…that's living in NYC for them.
That's the NYC they introduced to their girls…plus Anthony @

Johnnies.

The did their best to show the greatest spots from coast to coast, plus a little desert experience too. More than not, they were a beach family. But, anywhere hot, sunny, and with a pool or nice body of water would do. The islands and Gulf coast were tops, but there was nothing wrong with the Camelback Inn in Paradise Valley, AZ, close to their friends and business partners. What an escape! Who knew that the desert could be that beautiful and quite the hot refuge for them and many from 4-season climates. When not vacationing at their favorite resort, they stayed with JB and Gina at their wonderful homes, one early that was smaller, but sweet with a cool pool, and the next, larger one with a larger lagoon pool/outdoor recreation center and huge patios. It was a playground for all ages. Picture the centerpiece of a huge pool surrounded by rock and freeflowing waterfalls. To your left is the basketball court and trampoline.

To the right is the playground complex and a lawn of perfect grass. Back near the home is the pitch and putt course that crosses the entire back yards. Tees, greens, and sand traps. Multiple "holes" and just fun to play in the back yard. Oh, and the grill and patio seating and aguamisters that keeps everyone cool just hanging out with a beer and/or enjoying dinner.

Everyone has a pool out there, it seems. And, big walls to keep out the riff-raff and neighbors from peeking in. That was different too, but typical. That's how most roll in the SW desert states.

Mornings there were golden. Hot, but coffee on the patio with the newspaper and great "business" conversations were the norm. Take a dip when the heat builds up, maybe chip and putt and bit, off to breakfast, since neither of his hosts liked to cook much. This was a normal business day for them that always felt like a vacation. He would never have such a relaxed, productive, and enjoyable business experience ever again. Never.

Their media business was slowing down, facing increased competition for media time, and media rates were climbing. They tried like mad to diversify, but always seemed to have one big whale swimming in profitability while other little guppies just offered a break-even or win/loss from week to week. The split with the boys in Maine was for the best, but he and his team were on their own. A new office helped, but he missed that cozy basement on Needles Drive. He found it necessary to travel to their new call center and fulfillment house a couple of times a year. Not a problem. Napa Valley and San Fransisco were new adventures too. Very few places beat those places to eat, drink, and be merry.

They made the most of those times out there too. His Love would fly out and the Napa & Sonoma wine experiences were enjoyed. JB and Gina even joined them in San Fran for an amazing vacation there. They even stayed in that really nice hotel where President Reagan stayed years before. Maybe a Ritz or a Westin. He really cannot recall, but he does remember the street artists on the square and the cable car too, right outside the hotel's front door. No matter. It was cool. Love to visit, but could never afford to live there over the long run. And, that was a preGoogle/Apple/Microsoft boom era…unreal.

Their business was about to take a big turn. Their diet pill, that soaked up fat and sent it flying out of the body via shellfish fibers, had carried them for a while. Especially, when they decided to package 90-day Especially, when they decided to package 90-day day money-back guarantee. No questions asked.

That really worked until the big box retailers caught wind of this product and knocked it off for far less than $1 a day. He learned fast that, in this business, you have 6-18 months to make the most of your product sales with little to no competition. Others will always catch up. It's just a matter of time. He didn't help matters much when he shared their secret of the business with a future competitor. He learned something about a shrewd Jewish entrepreneur. Lesson learned, for the young Gentile.

Then, one day, an old friend reached out and wanted to meet with an old doctor he had met, probably through his Rotary Club or some other old fart networking group. He agreed to meet at their downtown club, top floor of the tallest building in their little hometown. He dreaded that meeting. The new character wasn't even a real doctor. He was a chiropractor. A kooky one, too. What could possibly become of this waste of time? Well. A lot.

Like many other product pitches, he sat back and let the old fella go. He prattled on for hours and he challenged what he could. His "fountain of youth" story was compelling and he certainly seemed like a great guest for a show, but his claims could be more than problematic or they could be super profitable…or both. He was convincing and charismatic too. He had to go back and convince his two partners that this was worth pursuing.

JB was cool, as always. His founding partner, Tom, was tougher to convince. He worked out all of the product logistics and negotiated the product pricing and contract, while Doc and Tom created a fantastic radio show to test. As with every show, after long edit sessions, this show was a good as it could be. Always sounding live, but always taped and airing at all hours of day and night across North America. Their test weekend approached and they were ready to see how a great test buy of $2-3k would or would not pay off.

Then, the call came in. Tom was not convinced that this would work and wanted him to pull the test and insert other profitable shows. He ignored that. The test went on. It's what they do. Test. Kill. Roll-out. Let the market decide, not just one person, even Tom. And, roll-out they did. That small test resulted in over $10,000 in sales the first weekend. It was a whale, as opposed to a guppy. Profitable from day one. Just imagine how profitable it could be with repeat sales, auto-shipments, and expanded media buys. His best act of business defiance ever.

That's how the business rolled on for a few more years. One whale climbs and spikes and another eventually takes its place…until it just doesn't.

Things were rocking a rolling. Sure, the Y2K and tech bubbles burst and cost him about $250k in stock market losses, but his business and income was taking off, along with his future "dream" home that lasted just a while. They just should have stayed in where they were or another cool spot and paid cash for everything. Woulda. Coulda. Shoulda.

His business moved again, into another affordable spot next to their CPA, which was nice. He hated going into the office with little to nothing to do, that did not involve a phone, email, or a fax machine. Thus, he stopped going into the office. If he was needed, they called or emailed his trusty Blackberry phone. He loved that great phone. No need to show up and kill time in the office anymore.

It was his greatest paycheck…freedom. He and his Love and their girls could travel or at least be free to go get them on their weekends and live it up. Their income, thanks to generous, quarterly profit-sharing, grew as much as their freedom. A win-win, it seemed.

Their new home under construction was coming along, after a brief cash-flow break, and it was becoming a monster of a home and a massive project.

His first of a two nervous breakdowns came during construction. He was in over his head and he knew it. JB came to his rescue, which he will never forget. But, he knew that he had to finish what he started, one way or another and the cash just kept coming his way. He even bought his first new ride in forever, a Lincoln Navigator. Zero down, zero interest, over 60 months. Done. It was a sweet ride and took care of their family of 4 + Bud quite well.

They got away on a train trip that Labor Day weekend with several other couples. They all drove down to Atlanta to catch the Amtrak train to the Big Easy.

They had to drive down, since no passenger train lines come close to their little hometown. They arrived and were quickly told not to park in the Amtrak parking lot, if they want to see their vehicle again. They were all guided to the skanky motel across the bridge from the station.

There, an interesting fellow behind the desk will take your keys and, for a nightly fee, will watch your vehicle investments. He parked his brand-new Navigator between his friend's Mercedes and Volvo. Maybe that luxury sandwich may just work. It did.

The Amtrak experience was exceptional. Granted, he felt the need to get everyone upgraded to sleeper cars, which comes with privacy and included, fancy meals. A tough, female conductor eventually came around and helped the privileged couples get comfortable after the parking drama. The staff was great and hilarious. He had never been surrounded by so many black people, stewards and other staff, in such tight spaces. They were like old friends he never had. They joked. They kept the couples advised about meal times and clued them in about getting their tables in time. The food was great. The rolling atmosphere and visuals outside were amazing. It was another first and they loved it. It wasn't Maui, where he and his love honeymooned and spent their 5-year anniversary the year before. However, the 10-hour or so ride to New Orleans was fantastic.

Fun friends and fun conversations are hard to beat, plus the privacy and rocking motion nap-ability made it even better. After a lot of fun, they arrived and hailed a few taxis to head into the Big Easy.

Let the good times roll. Their friend and "host", Marty, had planned out the long weekend to the nth degree. They all even had lanyards with itineraries and contact info, in case one got drunk and lost and some nice stranger could read off his or her contacts and destinations. It was funny, but very practical. Needless to say, they did not stick to the itinerary.

First thing, the next day, was Mother's. Mother's for breakfast was a must. A downtown anchor, nowhere near to tourist traps, was their target for their first breakfast.

Lots of beautiful, deep south, black women cooking up and doing business…not a man in sight. The line was long. It was well worth the wait. The ladies were fun and yucked it up with them. They loved him and he made the most of those brief conversations and laughs. He learned about "debris" from these seasoned cooks. It's the roast beef pieces that drop off the roast as it cooks. It's just that good. So good. His mouth waters just thinking about what those sweet ladies dished up that morning.

Cafe' Dumond, of course. A must for every human.

Jazz and original art on every square and a lot of street corners. He loved experiencing live talent that he mostly absorbed via his Bose stereo and original artwork hanging in their home. Now, it was in their face, ears, and big eyes. Beautiful New Orleans!

And, the food was on it's own too. Remember, they loved mid-town Manhattan and found lots of food and fun to love. But, the creole-infused, jazz-centric Big Easy became a new grown-up love…not so kid-friendly…but very cool for adults looking for varying degrees of fun and deliciousness.

As for the most delicious, their host booked dinner for all at Commander's Palace, in the Garden District. One of the greatest meals of all time, he still believes. They had all virtually died and gone to culinary heaven. They took cable cars back and forth and there were horse-drawn everything around the district. What's not to love about New Orleans?

Their weekend was capped off with a walk down Bourbon Street, in broad daylight, where he had his ass squeezed a bit by one flamboyant fellow in the parade, and he responded with an elongated "eaaassssy" right next to his Love. It was Decadence Weekend, aka gay pride weekend, and this party of hetero's had no clue about that. It was a hoot. The parade was fun and there were lots of banana hammocks and other "Big Easy" collateral around, but, alas, they had a train to catch back to Hotlanta.

Before heading home, he and his Love did indulge their love of art and frequent the galleries up and down Royal Street. Many nice art galleries and a few tiny ones that just get by. Then, there was Juanita. His name was John, but he wanted to be called Juanita. They interrupted him and his other half sucking face in the doorway of their "gallery", a roughly 10' x 10' space with three walls full of artwork.

He locked in on the largest piece there, with a gaudy, huge, gold-leaf frame, that was an original oil about an unknown NOLA jazz set. A 5 piece set. Just beautiful.

$5k later, it was being shipped back home for their new monster home to come. Not their first collector rodeo. They accumulated lots of local artist originals, giclee's, and a few prints too. They bought pieces at auction, to benefit local non-profits and they also found pieces by the one and only Chuck Jones, in Laguna Beach, that brought a little Looney Tunes art into their loony tune world.

Their trip home was full of more laughs, great food, and needed naps. New Orleans is exhausting and worth every dime and minute. Their vehicles were still there and that new Navigator had not budged, thanks to the nice fellow watching it. The happy couple returned home and decompressed a bit from another wonderful getaway to a new experience. But, he unpacked and, one week later, he had to repack for his next trip back to Scottsdale on Tuesday, 9/11/2001.

His Love reminded him about the dinner they had the night before he left for AZ. They were invited to meet a new chef and share a meal at one of their favorite local spots. In short, a nice meal was nearly spoiled by a heated conversation with the young, jerk chef who chose to lecture the wrong couple about the meaning of life. Chef and his wife were going to take a break from each other and he just kept inserting both feet in his mouth, as he and his Love kept giving it back to him…"life is too short and tomorrow is not a guarantee" was his Love's point to that little chef. Little did any of them know what was going to happen the very next morning.

Just like any other flight and trip, right? Just pack up and get where you are going. Just another beautiful Tuesday morning, it seemed. His Love takes him to the airport. He boards very early.

He flies to Atlanta, changes planes, and finds his spot there in first class…he ran the company and his AMEX took good care of him. Early drink in hand, probably a screwdriver, to calm the nonexistent nerves. All is well.

The plane takes off, as usual, and gets close to it's proper altitude when the stewardess comes over the intercom. "…the pilot will be making an announcement soon…" or something like that was shared. It took about 10 minutes for the pilot to get informed and relay his information to the entire plane. Another drink, por favor!!! Liquid courage was certainly needed as that day proceeded. The pilot announced an attack on NYC and that every single plane in America has been ordered to land immediately. After a bit of shock wore off, he leaned over to his mucholder seat mate and offered "well, there must be an attack with planes or landing them all makes no sense" or the like. Sadly, it was all too true. No trip to AZ. They quickly landed in Memphis.

First off the plane, those few first class privilege set made way to the Delta Crown Room, where the 9/11 horror unfolded. Grown men and women sobbing or crying as they watched everything unfold live on television or in replay. It was as shocking as anything can be when it's not you in the middle of the horror.

They were all bystanders, but deeply affected. Nowhere near Manhattan, but all hearts ached like they were there. Their plane wasn't a part of the horror, but it could have been. But, it was not. Four planes were and they watched the pure evil in action and pure heroes take one down in PA. Air Force One even circled the country with big firepower on each wing that day. It was an unbelievably, horrible day that made him cry more than a few times. A 33-year old husband and father of 2 that was reduced, not for the first or last time, to a puddle.

He bolted out of that airport, after getting terrible vibes from the understandably, clueless Delta staff, to find the only on-site, airport hotel. He passes a limo with a sign that offers to take anyone anywhere for $1,000….sad. He walked into the Radisson and secured the last room available. All planes were grounded indefinitely. He needed a place to get away, preferably with a pool…and that's what he had found. Tiny room. Nice pool. And, he's not dead.

An old friend was the first one he could reach and asked to contact his Love and all that matter. He did. His partners were trying to reach him too and all were assured that he was on the ground and all was relatively well.

His Love drove hours to get him the next day, since flights were not taking off for days and he would not pay criminals to drive him home.

9/11 did change everything…again. To the minute, as I write this, it's 14 years since that moment of change and devastation that shook the country and the civilized world. A somber memorial service is live on the television as I type this. It all kinda comes back, even all of these years later.

The country lost over 3,000 souls and he knew none of them. His only connection was the fact that he had eaten at the Windows on the World restaurant…that was it. Yet, the attack was so painful. He cannot imagine the degree of pain for those who died or lost their loved ones.

Out of the ruble over the next few days, everyone began to recover a bit, get angry, follow the lead of the new Texan president and get to rebuilding and showing the world what we were made of. It's still a work in progress.

What was also in full progress was the creation of their so-called "dream home". They were enjoying the last year in their cool, little neighborhood. Cook-outs, walks, and parties that would never be duplicated again.

After surviving the tech stock bubble, the Y2K scare, one of the most divisive national elections ever, new wars in the Middle East, and 9/11 all in a span of a couple of years, they needed a daily getaway and he intended to create just such a home destination for his family, friends, and those needing to gather and raise money for great causes they supported.

The home was massive, taking 18 months to design and another 18 to build. The largest dry-stack stone home anywhere around happened. 12,500sf under roof, with garages for their three vehicles, including a 1969 Cadillac convertible they bought years ago, and for their small fleet of golf carts. Seems ridiculous today. Add it to the list.

They held on to their first home and let his older brother live there, until that just didn't work anymore. Long, boring story there. They also owned another home up the street that helped a great friend and her daughter out for a time. Now, it was time to finish their home and use it for great gatherings and just live it up.

His remarkable financial success was only matched by his hubris and selective generosity. He and his Love returned a great sum of money back into their community through church and through certain non-profits.

He was asked to join various boards and met many fascinating and interesting folks that way.

He thought that his plan was sound. Pay cash for everything, as you can. Take out the loan, for tax purposes, when completed and pay off that loan in a few years. However, their $700-800k budget eventually ballooned to a $1.3million investment and a work of art, inside and out. A huge fish in a very tiny pond, much like his ego.

Little did he know that the remarkable gravy train was about to slow down and much bigger priorities were coming in just a couple of years. Best laid plans, as they say.

That first Christmas in the "big house" was magical. Many gatherings. Lots of fun and lots of people. Both girls now had their own rooms, plus a bonus room and another guest room upstairs. He and his Love had plenty of space to live and love, including a huge master suite, an office, a gourmet kitchen, a separate guest suite, and that sunken den and open floor plan he dreamed of as a kid.

Now was the time to try growing their family. His Love could now afford to take time off from her career to focus on growing their family. But, first, they needed to find someone to reverse what was done years before, after his girls were born.

He was snipped back then and needed the best in the country to fix the connection. He was referred to the best guy available and he was based in Texas.

Road trip! Over a few days of surgery and recovery, they were back and ready to grow their family again. Dr. Lipshultz wasn't cheap, but he was successful. His swimming boys were back, so to speak.

His Love, who is planning her own book regarding their path through infertility called "Fresh Eggs Ahead".

It was quite the road and she will explain her side of that journey someday. His side of it was simple. They were happy with their girls, but not the part-time parenthood. After months of trying, it just wasn't working. They went trough two different doctors, dozens of shots, medical /IVF procedures, and even suffered through a heart-breaking miscarriage. His reversal and her procedures and shots seemed to be anything but reproductive…a little infertility humor there.

All of the prayers in their worlds, plus multiple medical professionals could not offer them the chance to expand their family and fill that huge home with more love and life everyday.

Almost a year after they moved in, they broke away and headed back to NYC with their friends and business partners. It was a long weekend full of laughs, shows, and great food…plus Nostrovia! Who knew that the cure for infertility was simply a Russian vodka bar near Times Square. They ended most nights there, before retiring to their hotel nearby. Picture a long, shotgun bar with jar after jar of vodka-soaked fruits, peppers, and other edible things. Their tastings worked. About 9 months later, their baby boy was born. His Love had a pleasant pregnancy and she was able to take the time needed to care for herself and her new love. His Love was a gorgeous mom-to-be and hasn't really changed since. She is still a remarkable beauty, inside and out. Nostrovia!

Just loosen up, you folks of a certain age, and things just happen. And, great things did happen. They continued to travel. The discovered SW Florida and fell in love with Captiva Island and its family businesses.… Jensen's, the Mucky Duck, and the Bubble Room…fun places. The clincher was the small, beachside church that they attended that Easter.

A sweet, welcoming congregation in a perfect beach setting. They even stumbled upon the church's historical book titled "In God's Time". The irony of that title was not lost on them, as they were finally pregnant and working towards a comfortable summer before their boy arrives.

One last trip for a while, back to the Gulf Coast. They booked a different home each year and brought all grandparents down too. Great beach time, walks, seafood, naps, and laughs over bingo and other games. His dad would always call out the bingo numbers with a tumbler contraption. They always cooked or went to dinner early, in order to have lots of family time every evening. The next summer's trip will have one extra member there. Baby's first beach. Love it. In God's time…

That fall, they settled in with their newborn and got their girls down to be with them as often as possible. It was a great time. A few more years and many holiday seasons to go, before life takes yet another turn.

In the meantime, they were even able to send both sets of grandparents to Hawaii on separate trips, thanks to SkyMiles, just as they were sent there years before.

God blessed their family with many things and ability to help many and, also, spoil themselves. God's greatest blessings, healthy children, kept coming too. Life just kept getting better…which he believes is just when you should be prepared for the downturn to come. And, it came.

Life is cyclical like that. Now, a family of five with a huge home full of love, art, and comfortable spaces…but, absolutely over-the-top and too much space for even a family of 5 and, eventually, 6. He just realized that way too late. Again, hubris and ego trumped common sense and practicality that he allowed to leave his head. He had to figure out how to counter the sales and profitability decline and pay the bills with his declining income. Of course, he wanted to keep their family traveling too and they headed to Turks & Caicos, the summer between the birth of each baby boy. It was their 10th wedding anniversary trip and this one was shared with their three kids, in that allinclusive way. It was a great trip and the last one like that for a while.

The beginning of an end of excess was near. He was sitting on his back deck, reading his local newspaper, back when he did such things, and his phone rings. It was their internet pro out in AZ and great friend of JB and Gina. He got right to it. JB and Gina, their new guard dog, and co-pilot, Terry, had been in San Diego, where they owned an airplane hanger/condo near downtown. As they left to fly themselves back to Scottsdale two days before, they his rough weather and slammed into a "thumb" or rock outcropping, which destroyed their plane and killed all on-board.

Their remains were found strewn through the mountain desert just east of San Diego. Both men on the phone lost it. He shook. He paced the deck and eventually had to sit down. His friends and business partners were dead. So was part of him. So was the future of the business, it seemed.

Things were never really the same again.
The next ten years begin....

Two tween girls. One little dude. Another one on the way. And an amazing Love that stuck with him through a deep depression that still rears its ugly head for years afterwards. And, she's still there. Propping him up. Defending him, as needed. And, most of all, caring for and loving him, even when most women would scream and eventually give up. She was and is his gift from God. He knows that, even at his lowest points.

They made one last happy trip to Scottsdale when their boy was only a baby. This last sad trip happens that fall with current and former business partners and they stay, as JB would, at the Ritz-Carlton. They reminisced and enjoyed the beauty of the place, just like JB and Gina's home. They were now gone and the "celebration of life" , as they called it, was probably just what they would have wanted. It was sweet, sad, and the close to another part of his and his Love's life. He visualized, and still does today, those two friends and partners going down the sidewalk and street...busy streets...Gina on her roller-blades and JB on his Segway vehicle. Quite the funny and surreal sight. Welcome to the sunny Arizona.

This cool man, JB, became his friend and his mentor in a way no other business associate had. It just didn't last too long. That relationship should have been over decades, not just short of one decade. Gina was pure joy. She was petite, but very muscular. Strong in more than one way. She was as funny and magnetic as a girl from Chicago could be. She didn't care about the big money and stuff. She still volunteered in old folks homes and tried to get them to move and be healthy. She loved kids more than anyone without kids of her own could. She was just joy, almost like a tv character…but, she was very real, very fun, very self-deprecating, and just someone you wanted to be around, as often as possible. She was quite younger than JB and that's just what he needed. Sweet and not a typical young gal…again, pure, genuine, joy. That was Gina.

They also had a huge, loving family that stretches from their hometown in AZ to Chicago. Lots of family and friends. Lots of love. A degree of functional family and friends the likes he had never experienced.

That made his trips to AZ that much more special and wonderful. People hugged. They kissed. They actually gathered on a regular basis and enjoyed their company. Not his family experience. He and his Love had many friends and they gathered from North Hills to the Big House to other places, but the AZ experience was different and special. And, it was finished.

His last memory of those two were their ogling over their new baby boy and Gina rolling around on the carpet with him taking pictures of this cute little blob that could not walk or even sit up yet. He and his Love never saw those pictures and that is so sad.

One ironic memory that sticks with him today is where JB went on and on about how safe the skies were, relative to the interstate, and how he should just get his pilot's license, buy a plane too (another lousy investment), and go get his girls in a half an hour, not 3 hours or so each way. JB made a great case, as only a long-time pilot could, but his gut said no. No confidence nor risktolerance for such a hobby or vocation. JB never got it. It was another reason why they just got along so well. They were almost different generations and were a good balance in the company. JB was brilliant and had instincts he could only pray for. He never quite got there. He almost gave up on such.

He was beginning a long road to his next era of fatherhood, husbandry, and trying to help other entrepreneurs fulfill their personal and business potential. It worked well, for a while.

He saw the reality to come. He listed their dream home and the showings began. Gotta dump this cash cow and restart elsewhere. They needed a "big fish" for this little pond, which could be a doctor or lawyer or business owner who wanted the nicest work of livable art available in their little town. No such luck. The holidays were fun, as usual, and just blew by. Lots of wine and cocktails helped, for sure. Life became a bigger and bigger blur.

The next year, here came another boy. He was perfect, too. Two healthy girls and two healthy little dudes. Screw the dream home. They kept plugging along, dipping into their substantial retirement fund and kept the fun rolling along. Sure, they had their own personal resort home, including a dry sauna in the master bath…nice…five fireplaces, a great kitchen and gathering places. But, they even briefly lost their oldest boy in that massive home. That was a wake up call, to say the least.

More dinner parties and fund-raisers rolled on, plus a tv show produced by HGTV, a black-tie affair with a bunch of friends..and a few slept over between couches, bedrooms, and the guest suite. It was a fun night, but the show was a pain in a way…fun being directed is not so fun.

It was a new year and time to dust off that BS degree and get those entrepreneurial juices flowing again. Buzzing up and down the interstate to get his girls, he noticed a unique business related to the golf world. Golf was his only "sport". He joined the club next door and also bought his parents and in-laws their own memberships. They shared lots of great meals, pool parties, and, of course, golf with their family there. The club put the "country" in country club, but it was fine. Great course. Great food. Great bar. And, all just a short cart ride away from home.

Back to business, the world's largest golf cart accessory business was his new interest. He stopped in a shopped a couple of times and eventually asked to meet the owner. A short, bundle of energy, much like his former partner in the last business, and one that knew what he wanted..perfection from everyone. This was his third fellow of this ilk that he seemed to be drawn to or they were drawn to him. Who knows? Those two did hit it off. He invited his new friend and his wife down to his home to play golf, enjoy the kids, and cook up some great food. They did come down and stay and they created a business relationship at that time, as well. They had a consulting agreement for a decent annual fee, plus expenses.

He would be there weekly, while his Love stayed home with their boys, offering on-site assessments of the various parts of the organization and advise the owner and his CFO about their strong and weak links and possible changes to make. Like his former business, there were too many family fingers in the pot and that's why he was now there. It was a tough gig. The way its always been is the way its always to be, so entitled family and friends of the business may think. His style was pretty non-threatening, although his physique may have been to some. He just came in and met everyone in the building one person at a time. Sure, there were lots of folks on the front-lines taking sales calls or fulfilling orders, which he knew a lot about, but could not critique at any level. It was the management that needed to be known…and the cook…a fantastic cook who whipped up free lunches everyday for the staff. This guy was an amazing cook and was also the owner's driver and took the limo out so the boss would not risk a DUI after time at his club or another haunt. Smart, but over the top, but that's how that entrepreneur friend rolled and he liked it.

Like always, this was a fun ride. Lots of positive energy, very nice meals, and great booze. Does any decent business relationship need any more?

Both men really had an affinity for wine and bourbon, not to mention great steaks. Both enjoyed a casual round of golf too. For the first time in a while, it seemed, his Marketing and Sociology degree seemed to be directly paying off like he was sold in business school.

Golf, booze, red meat, and all of the accouterments, plus another expense account. He was kinda back…for a while. He even went that extra distance and opened up a custom golf-cart business of his own and you know who his main supplier was. Not good. Lesson learned….again.

Both men, plus the owner' VP of Operations/older brother even travelled together in the big car to the Villages of central Florida, the mecca of retiree golf and golf cart shuttle living, where over 50,000 golf carts and residents roam the lush landscape and small "downtown" areas. That was the place for a custom cart store, but they weren't uprooting to Florida just yet.

(The Villages community is also a hot bed for hot beds too, evidently. An STD capital for old people, it seems. That was an icky tip they learned on that particular road trip)

That was quite the business road trip, educational in more ways than one. All three drank more than they should. He played referee between the two stubborn brothers.

It was quite the ride, but he seems to be very gifted in wild rides and attracting or being drawn to interesting characters. That lasted for a while, but everything does have its life in the business world. Entrepreneurs who relish control, especially with the checkbook, and also have ego's and personalities are frequently not positioned well for long-term success and profitability. He learned this lesson over and over again, until he just could not take it anymore a few years later.

In business, it's all about what you've done for us lately. Not loyalty. Not intent. Not sacrifice. Not any of the 10 Commandments. Not even customer or client satisfaction. Just what have you added to the bottom line lately. That's it. An MBA in just one, short paragraph.

His ride on that golf cart ended and his little custom golf cart business folded to that same year. He had managed to sell over $300k in product, but it was not sustainable. He was used to much bigger profit margins and not sweating quite as much. He did it all alone and he folded it up alone, except for the time the family stepped up and helped him build a fleet of carts for a local course. That was surreal and sweet. They did not have to do that, but they did. He'll never forget that effort and that love for his crumbling soul.

He now had many years of sales, marketing, and management success under his belt, but not a very convincing resume' to market his skills. No one was reaching out. No real help at all. You reap what you sew, it seemed. He reached out to others, but did not plant his own seeds of future contacts and opportunities. It was amazing how his expertise in managing a multi-million dollar business just did not translate. He did not want to join corporate America and that ladder climbing, but he was pushing 40 and on his own to figure this out yet again. And, he did again.

After about three years of listings, pricing from $2.1 million down to $1.3 million he had enough and they were done. His 40th birthday was approaching and they lined up the nicest, most positive and well-connected auctioneer they knew, Bear. Bear did everything that he could do. He promoted the hell out of that auction and he knew the number he had to hit. That Sunday, his 40th birthday, arrived and some of the local vultures of the BAC swooped in their home. They wandered their home and eventually listened to Bear do his thing. By the end, as they sat on their sunken den hearth, he knew that it was all over. He instructed Bear to get all of these vultures out of his home and let's lock the door behind them. Bear did and a few tried to cut a lowball deal in the driveway. He had nothing to do with that. His auction and his birthday were collective busts and he just kept on planning. He informed his Love that they would hand over the keys to the bank before they surrendered their work of livable art to any vultures. And, that's exactly what they did, after planning their move and seamless departure from that place he grew to loathe.

He was as pissed off as a new 40-year old could be and his mentor and most trusted advisor was dead. He was done and so was the US economy for now.

The following week, Lehman Brothers fell, the Fed rescued what it could, and no one was in the mood to invest in a big home or in a big guy with tough to translate skillsets. He knew this.

He found a historic home back in North Hills, with extensive gardens and a lot of character and charm. They leased to own that home, but the character and charm wore thin as the 80-year old toilets flushed occasionally. Other upgrades were needed too and their old friends had all left the old neighborhood. Thus, they decided that maybe a downtown loft might be best for their family. He called an old friend and found the coolest condo ever on the 10th floor of an old bank building that two other friends made into the nicest downtown 2BR/2Ba home they had ever seen. It was cool, sleek, and very expensive. His Love returned to work as their boys headed towards pre-school and he had found his next entrepreneur to help out.

His contacts downtown led him to a young, creative firm with a brash, young owner who could use a seasoned someone to help grow his business. Their first meeting with tepid, at best, on the front porch of the historic, downtown spot. Again, only unique characters in this guy's life, it seems. Somehow, they made it work for a while.

He earned another fair income, brought in new business, and he tolerated the office atmosphere, banter, and bitch-fests from various grown men and women there, as long as he could. It was for his family. After a year or so, he left and that business fell apart too. They called it a sale, but he knew better. The business was propped up by very nice in-laws who funded it quite well and also had Chicago connections that offered even more funding. Good for them. It's great to know people and make great connections. He should know. He had not done such a g r e a t j o b f o r h i m s e l f a n d h i s f a m i l y . H i s recommendations for that business were not exactly welcomed and that very creative business "sold" soon after he left.

He focused on his non-profit board service, led one for a time, and was also nominated and allowed to serve in their local leadership society that recognized his service to charity. That was a great group of 40 or so. One year of traveling the area and meeting lots of good people too.

He and his Love did the fundraiser things and still gave away a lot of money. It's what they did, when the good times were rolling and even afterwards, it seemed. Life was short and he might have been damned determined to make it even shorter, if his drinking had any say in the matter.

He was embracing his inner New Orleans or Russian vodka bar or anywhere Caribbean …he could not help himself for a time.

The family loved their downtown condo. It was right there in the middle of it all, as much as they could be. And their new toilets actually flushed. Huge inside joke there, but easy to decipher. His Love just wanted flushing toilets and he made that happen in the new condo built for four. Watching swirling poop try to take a dive was not his Love's idea of entertainment. Their last morning in their last old home ended with a non-flushing poop incident that they still laugh about today.

There they were in an overpriced, high-floor loft condo that was very nice. Too nice… and so nice for all four kids and their aging pup, Bud. It even came with a part-time doorman, Richard. He was very sweet. man and he became their friend too. packages and groceries, when they needed him. He'll never forget his first, and probably last, doorman. He was a jewel.
He was a special

He helped with

Those downtown years were wonderful. They walked to pre-school at their church and eventually both boys to elementary school via Miss Denise and her school bus that picked up their boys every morning around 7am at the historic theatre across the street from their building.

Quite the nice bus stop. Downtown was quite a different community. lots of empty nesters, downtown workers, and a few families with kids…and thousands of visitors a few nights every month. They walked everywhere and that was a highlight of their downtown experience.

His Love's sales career was back to rocking and rolling. He had sold all remaining property and other liquid holdings from previous investments and businesses and he could take a break to see what to pursue next. Opportunities still proved few and far between for him, justified or not.

He was burned out on the local non-profit world too. Too many hands out and too much overlap or redundancies in the 2,000+ non-profits of this little town. Not a place for a business guy who thought consolidation and greater efficiency was the answer to the services offered to those who needed it most. Slash the overhead and even the board size per mission… those would never happen or he did not have the charisma to make it happen or both. Too many hands in those respective pots to let common-sense over-rule self-interests. It's a common theme in every organization he crossed paths with.

That was and is his biggest roadblock/career issue. He's ruled out 90% or more of corporations, which could never get his resume' and 100% of redundant and inefficient non-profits…he has few viable options over 40 years of age and bitterness. Only a few friends and their family owned businesses would interest him enough to pursue. He consulted, helped a few friends, and was taken advantage of by some of them. They were scratched of his list too. The beginning of a much simpler life was here.

Christmas was coming and downtown retailers needed help. Nothing really interested him until he heard that the local "general store" needed holiday help. He applied and he was brought on-board for a few weeks. A few weeks that became 2 1/2 years. Meeting and greeting mostly complete strangers was his "job". Sure, he advised shoppers, was the unpaid tourism consultant to visitors, and also ran the register and took others money, as needed. It was fun, for a while. Never a dull moment during the holiday season.

Fairly dull otherwise, but just a couple of blocks from home. Going back to P&L's, various management accountabilities, and other demands were over. A simple job to do that never resulted in after-hours calls to home or any real responsibility for others welfare. Life became quite simple downtown.

Again, where things are going really well, a correction is on its way. Bud was now 14. HIs trips outside had become a bit disturbing. Things were not normal. He struggled He took forever to do his business. Then, there was blood. That's all he needed to head ASAP to his friend and vet. After her examination, she detailed that he had a mass and it was about the size of a small football. It was constricting his internal organs, which explained his discomfort and trips outside.

He was the best dog a family could have, anal glands and all. He was a car-sick pup that never travelled well, but he was pampered by their kennel owners every time they flew, drove, or sailed away for an extended time. Bud's last days were very comfortable. Bud had an elevator, a park, lots of smells, and lots of love in and out of the condo. But, one day, he could not function well and something had to be done. His system was being choked off and he needed relief. It was decided to give him that relief ASAP and end his pain. He drove Bud out to his vet and friends' farm.

It was and is a beautiful place on a hill. He led Bud out to a nice, westward, sunset slope of the property. Bud looked so peaceful. He dug Bud's grave. It took a while. Bud just sat and watched. After he was done, his friend and Bud's vet joined them. She had the medicine needed to put him to sleep.

They laid there with Bud, petting him, and, eventually, she injected the medicine and Bud looked up one last time…then, he fell asleep. 14 years of real love came to a melancholy close. His friend was as kind and generous as few had ever been over the last few years. He was so grateful and thinks fondly of Tracey to this day. Bud was special.

He slid his lifeless body into a heavy bag and placed him into his resting place. He said goodbye again and worked a little while longer to bury him in a way that no other animals would discover him.

It would be years before they found another perfect family pet and her name would be Lilly.

Death was beginning be the uncomfortable norm. Grandparents and great-grandparents were dying. A child of friends died. Others of their age dropped dead. Old age wasn't the only culprit. Divorce was taking hold too. It was their new era. Middle-age grabbed them by the jugular.

TIme for another getaway to the Gulf. BP motivated those summer vacations. For very little, they bought two weeks of vacation at the Gulf, tar balls and all. One week in June and another in July. No grandparents.

Just their kids and a fun two weeks helping the Gulf folks recover and just enjoying their place that BP almost destroyed.

Future summers took them back there and also back to Pass-A-Grille, Florida…their newest beach home. He was even able to share PAG with his oldest girl during her spring break and back to NYC for his youngest girl's spring break. Their choice and both were really fun..yes, two young and loved daughters wanting to spend their respective spring breaks with dad…really? The old man was very happy and his Love supported it all. She knew what the dad-daughter relationship was all about. He was happy. He was available. HIs lack of career must have had a deeper meaning.

He also loved the fact that their girls were starting to travel the world. They were not stuck in some hometown of any kind and he loved that so much. But, they still returned to spend time with their family, at every opportunity. Oh, and both girls earned full-scholarships to their private school…pretty darn impressive, he relished. More than well-rounded young ladies are they.

2013 brought one of those sad years of 3's . His maternal grandmother almost made it to 100 years of age, but passed just short of that.
A few months later, a saint of a man, his father-inlaw, passed away in his 80's, and, that July, at the age of 78, his own father gave in to the trials of Alzheimers, diabetes, and other issues…and he, too, left them.

His grandmother was that sweet cook, mother, grandmother, and fan of baseball. His father-in-law was a Dartmouth graduate, a decorated Navy chaplain and Commander, a great husband, a loving father, and neverreally a retired pastor. He was amazing and he is still missed. His dad was all that was detailed earlier, but especially a unique man, solitary kind of guy, and one that could never be duplicated…except by his youngest son, who feels more and more like his did everyday…sans the blue collar job and those likely experiences.

All were very sad deaths. All happened that one year.

His dad's death, fortunately, came quickly that July. It was the British Open, or "The Open" as they call it, weekend. He went to the hospital that Thursday when his dad was admitted with complications. They watched their last British Open together that night and his dad knew who some of the players were. All was under control. Friday was uneventful and he did not visit his dad. Saturday morning came and his mom called.

He raced to the hospital and he missed him passing by a ten minutes. He kissed his forehead and it was slightly cool. Dad was gone. He sat down and held his hand while giving his mom a break and he watched the 3rd round of the British Open on tv. It was a fitting last hour with his dad. Very fitting. Golf was one of their few connections. In God's time, as they say.

His dad's shuffling between his bedroom and the sunroom was over. His getting lost on the road was over some time ago. His sleeping for 18+ hours a day was over. His handful of daily pills to take was over. His long goodbye was over.

Living from moment to moment and no real recollection of where he just was or names of loved ones was over. His dad's life was now over.

His dad did teach him a few things about living in the moment. Alzheimers demands it, if you're smart and listen. Go to their place, not yours. Go to their reality, not yours. Never quiz about the past. Just be in the present. His dad never forgot who his son was, which was a cherished blessing. His dad always greeted him with the same fun tone, big smile, and welcoming words and he tries to do the same with his kids when they walk in the door.

His dad still did not tell him that he loved him, though. His dad just said "me too" whenever his son offered a "love you" to his dad. Mothers Day, birthdays, and other holidays were non-issues, since his dad forgetting those became bigger opportunities for stress that his dad could not handle. They celebrated in other places and his dad did not have to know. He gave up Father's Day too. Too painful. His dad had no chance of remembering any holiday or birthday, let alone how to buy gifts or cards.

He just asked his dad "How are you?" and the like. It was simple and sent the conversation wherever his dad wanted to go. That's just as it should be.

Visits were few that last year. It was too depressing and his dad would not remember past a few minutes anyway. His dad went to the hospital for the last time, weak and confused and unusually ornery. He could still recall details of decades past, but not names, places, and happenings of earlier today.

That last year offered him tremendous opportunity for self-reflection, as it pertained to his middle-age and how he wanted to invest the remainder of his life, let alone how he did not want to end it. His dad was never short of opinion and comment and that was completely hereditary.

He decided to journal such opines and thoughts for his own catharsis and for his loved ones to eventually absorb someday. His Love and his children and close friends would have a written record of his thoughts of his half-life so far, including a big change in how he practices his faith.

His catharsis began here….back up to April 1st, 2012.

"Who really NEEDS the church today?"

"I loathe New Years resolutions, even more than promises sparked by Lent. Is it just a coincidence that, about 100 days into my church-free existence, I awoke at 1am or so with my mind racing about putting this part of my journey to virtual paper…on Palm Sunday?

Let me back up a few months. Just after the blitz and wonder of this past Christmas Season, I imagined what my little world would be like without our church, the very impressive and artistic creation of many men and women. A place where My Love and I were married. A place where our 4 kids grew up and/ or are still doing so. A place full of good people doing good to great things everyday. Also, a place that I just don't need anymore. It was not planned. I just said goodbye and kept it to myself…until now.

Like healthy food and clean water, we need a faith in something bigger than us to live well. Something that inspires us to overcome our normal, human condition. Something that just keeps our eyes and ears open to daily opportunities to make a positive difference in our small world. I do believe in God, his Son, and what Jesus is said to have accomplished 2,000+ years ago. As for man's creations for worship, I'm just over it. Is it just me? Is it my age? Is it just another "dare to be different" moment in my life? Or, is this feeling a new dawn on a new era for the last half of this one life? I wish that I knew for sure very…but my very public effort here will attempt to source wisdom, constructive feedback, and help me explain my journey's foundation to my wife, my kids, and to anyone who gives this effort any time, insight, and energy."

He was searching for some solitude and he started that process to divest himself of people and places that did not give him the peace he needed moving forward.

Then, he went on one day later…

"…the river is my church."

"Those were the words offered by my massage therapist years ago at the Camelback Spa in Scottsdale. Like my bloated expense account back then, I was grateful for, yet humored by, her words of wisdom. With my face squished into the padded ring thing, I simply retorted "well, who do you think made the river?", which was followed by the usual awkward silence. I get that a lot. Hey, I'm an outdoor guy. I heart the local greenways, regional mountains & streams, and, most of all, our beaches of the Gulf coast. All a part of a really big, complicated creation by a pretty

amazing higher power. My much-older, husky, East German Olympian masseuse did not accept the connection…or so she said. I've thought about that conversation for years.

Maybe considering the river as a place of worship IS just as valid as the love and care given to a stone, marble, and wooden shrine to God. Maybe. It just seems to me that there's a balance somewhere between the little wooden church in the country and the Crystal Cathedral in California, which was recently foreclosed by the Shular family's lenders.

My own church had a multi-million $$$ capital campaign for a beautiful building that demanded repair and preservation for decades to come. Done. The church that I finished my childhood in built a mega-church years ago, with an aging congregation, and stresses today under several million dollars of debt. Thus, country to city, old to new, aging to new congregation…bigger is better? Well, there's nothing bigger than creation. Maybe my snarky response to that lady kneading me like a 275-pound lump of dough was foolish. Maybe she was wise and at the very place that I find myself today. Funny.

Every group of like-minded folks need a place to gather together, rain or shine. For some, it's that neighborhood hang-out. For some, it's the grocery and Walmart. For some, it's the golf course or country club. For many, wealthy to not-so, faithful to not-so, young to not-so, genuine to not-so…it's the Church. Once or twice a year to every few days, millions of Americans gather with like-minded (exc politics) folks to worship, socialize, exercise, feed our kids minds & souls, and God only knows what else. It is the modern church. It works for most or it wouldn't exist. My rhetorical question is "when is the church just a church?". I've joked for years about two types of churches. One is just a church, which can be large or small. The other is the church of "what's happening now", with big-screen TV's, big technologies, family life centers, gymnasiums, etc. Sure, there are hybrids too and our church is one of then. So, make it 3 types, but that clutters up the joke.

I would love to know what God thinks about where we have taken the church in modern times. I hope to find out someday, when it's a little too late.

Maybe he's telling us now through the Shular family, through the debt-obsessed congregations, and through shrinking congregations and resources to fund the very real business side of organized religion. Although they never enjoy hearing it, all 4 of our kids have been target of my "it's never enough…just be thankful for what you DO have" one-liners to longer lecture. Sure, God is God and void of the snark + sarcasm that my kids expect from old Dad, but the point is made. From our home to our church-home, when is enough just enough? Is bigger really any better? If the river is your church, are you always looking for a bigger and better river? Shall we gather at the river, so to speak?"

He just could not go on as before and everyone will just need to understand. He continued to write about local and national issues, some interesting and some not at all….he continued the next day…

"We could always use one more, Allen."

"I'm a son of Alzheimers. At least it feels that way today. My Dad was a great athlete in his youth, became a local bowling and golf champion, worked an extremely varied working-class career, and sometimes helped Mom raise two boys. That's all pretty much history, but still educates me. He's now in his little world between the bedroom and the sunroof of the little rancher home where I grew up.

Dad was also a preacher's kid, who never voluntarily set foot in church after he left home, except for weddings and funerals. Papaw was a sweet, little, round grandad, preacher, and Barber of Vestal to me. Dad has shared other recollections in the past. The most telling memory he shared with me once has left me obsessed with making sure our kids know "I love you" from this Dad on a regular basis. Sounds easy for our generation. Not so much for the previous generations of Dads.

Mom, on the other hand, lives and breathes church. Always has…as long as I've known her. She probably needed it more, like many work/bowling/golf widows of that generation. She drug my brother and I too. My brother bolted early and probably never looked back at church, past his first marriage. Mom was a rock… practical, spiritual, and sarcastic all in one little woman frame. She still is for her church today. Church is her rock, it seems, and she needs it. Dad was diagnosed years ago with early stages of Alzheimer's disease. Not how one's retirement years should be spent. But, that for another day and a future eulogy.

Back to my Dad and his rare observation regarding organized religion. One story sticks out in my mind. One of the

life-long preachers I had as a kid would visit Dad at our home every few years. My best memory of one visit was when Preacher Holland was rhetorically slapped by my Dad with "church is just full of hypocrites". To which, this good preach retorted "well, we could always use one more, Allen". I still love that snappy comeback. The good preacher was ready for that one.

Every group in every part of our small worlds is full of hypocrites, intellectuals, fools, cool kids, grown-ups, and kids… like never REALLY left high-school. Why should the church be any different?

There are even clubs of like kids of similar demographics. We call the Sunday School classes. My

Dad's silly generalization still has merit with me…but…I would replace "hypocrites" with "humans". It's just the way it is and I'm not ready for any reunion…even this Holy Week."

And all of that was journaled in just the first three day of April, 2012. He was thinking a lot that week about what lies ahead. He was and is always thinking.

His older girls were away in a fantastic private university, where each had earned full scholarships for all four years. Brilliant girls that travelled the world and he could not be more proud of them, as he tried to detail here…

"Daughters and Dad"

"Regardless of gender, kids are just special. I honestly believe that nurturing, educating, and disciplining our kids, or

kids others have neglected, is our greatest adult challenge and opportunity for a better small to greater world. The greatest! Not everyone chooses or is able to have kids, but kids in need are almost everywhere around us and certainly are in the majority outside of America.

As for us, we have 4 very different kids in almost 2 different generations. 2 Millennial young ladies and two Gen? little dudes. Our little dudes' stories are barely unfolding now.

Our almost 20- & 18-year old girls are another story. From this Dad's perspective, they each have an amazing story already. Being a bit sensitive to their privacy, I will keep this a bit vague. Suffice it to say, each have been blessed with a loving family, a mix of family characters, a sense of humor, all they really need, a lot of wants too, and each has travelled the world like I never have. Not spoiled. Pretty grounded and appreciative. Both will go far and it's too exciting to watch each step as it happens. They each know that the world is so much bigger than any one home and hometown. Every kid needs that knowledge and perspective that he or she can get out and make a difference, which will make for a really purpose-driven life.

At the other end of life, I'm witnessing another Dad and daughter mix that I will never completely understand. It's complicated, sweet, and confusing. It makes me think about myself in my 80's, if I get there, and what my girls will think of this Dad and his life well-spent. Thus, with maybe four decades left, I'm a little obsessed about cheap thrills like making people laugh everyday to doing the same in one or more villages of the Caribbean and Central America someday. Plenty left to accomplish.

If you're a Dad, keep the faith, good priorities, and let the vanity go. We should just accept the fat and ugly as we grow old and show our kids and others what really living is. If you are not a Dad, go find that one kid or one group that helps lift kids up from whatever. It's just what real men should do.

By the way, kids, your old Dad really loves you."

Then, there was his Mom and his Love, three moms get a little love…

"Mom. Love her."

"Mom.

I started, like billions of boys, as a son. 19 years later, I'm a husband. 6 years and 2 beautiful girls later, I'm an ex-husband. Then, I'm saved by a Saint and made a husband again…plus 2 handsome boys.

Point is that I know Moms. My own. My first love. My lifelong love. I do know Moms.

Mothers Day is almost here. My mom has her sweets and tasty stuff from the General Store. All good. My Love, my much better half, will have her simple turquoise jewelry ensemble from the same store and our little boys will be proud of their giftgiving expertise via Dad.

We should all appreciate mothers. Any mother. I know one 25 year old boy who cannot appreciate his mom. I plan to rock her

world a bit this Mothers Day weekend… as best I can. All moms should remember this Sunday. As I cook and serve dinner for our 3 moms (my love, her mom, and mine) this Sunday, I'm going to think about those derelict sons out there and their moms. Please, find that mom near you and just do what you know is right."

Summer was upon him and he was feeling good about the times to come…

"It's halftime of this life…I hope."

" As a red-blooded, middle-age guy, I can interpret anything in life as a sports metaphor. Usually, baseball fits best, with curve balls, homers, foul balls, strikes, outs, wins, losses, fellow players, coaches, owners, egos, old and new fields of play…the epidemic of the human condition. However, there's no halftime in baseball…just a 7th inning stretch.

I feel like my halftime, Lord willing, is here. No actuary, astrologer, or scientist required. Just a hunch. Mid to late 80's is the guesstimate between my mom and Dad's bloodlines. This weekend reaffirmed my guess a bit.

We watched our youngest girl graduate from high school yesterday. Her journey so far has been a loving, intelligent, funny, adventuresome, and even relaxed one. Just like her sister, she is brilliant and "dares to be different", as I have challenged them over the years. Never settle. Never assume that you will be cared for by another. And just enjoy what you do have, instead of the

proverbial "grass is always greener on the other side" lifestyle. Strong, independent, thoughtful, and open-minded young ladies are these two. Very, very positive role models too for other kids of divorce…not to mention killer prep for picking their mate someday and making a lifelong marriage work.

Funny thing is…my lifelong love of 17+ years, so far, and I have two very different, little guys who are just beginning their journeys. One is the pleaser and over-achiever (just finished a 300+ page math workbook in 4 days) and the other is a bit more relaxed about such things. Deja vu, all over again. Our second half will be another interesting and adventurous time for all of us. However, we are older parent-players now. Wiser? Maybe so. Experienced? Certainly. In need and living a much simpler life?

Absolutely.
Simple living. Much less "stuff". Fewer bills to pay. Many more simple pleasures. Simple. We camped in the Great Smoky Mtns National Park as a family for the first time this week. Hiking. Cooking. Reading. Hammock lounging. Just being together.
Our halftime is about over, as we watch our oldest two kids take flight, with full academic scholarships to college in the bank. Who knows where they go from here…but I promise that each will make it interesting. Same for these little guys. Same for the best woman I've ever known, loved, and allowed to influence me more than any other, My Love.
Love. Get outside. Cook. Eat well. Imbibe. Laugh a lot. Cry a little. Just live. It's just that not-so simple…Lord willing."

After getting out of the business world, managing the downsizing of stuff, and purging other areas of life dissatisfaction , he resigned himself to being just another domestic god. He cooks, cleans, shuttles the kids around, writes, reads, and walks to keep his heart healthy and his waistline shrinking. He went from a size 44 to 38, or about 30 pounds, and it was a great thing. They moved to another condo near their boys school and life was simplified a bit more. He kept writing about the state of politics and was poked, by recent events in their life to write this…

"Men of a certain age. It's complicated."

"We've had our young couple years with like couples. We've enjoyed and are still enjoying raising two very different pairs of kids. And, now, these middle years bring us wave after wave of friends and acquaintances changing course in their respective journeys.

Most of the time, it seems to be guys behaving badly. Not always. Just most of the time. Again, it's complicated. What motivates a guy to go beyond everyday flirting to crossing a line with little to no return. I'm guessing that it's perceived leverage. Think about it. How many businessmen leave their wives for a younger associates? Doctors with their staff? Anyone with anyone seeking "greener grass"? It's all about leverage, at the workplace and at home. Bosses have it with staff. Bread-winners have it with so-called home-makers. Put the two together in environs of privilege…well…uber-leverage happens.

You know who I'm talking about. We all do, if your GenX or older. Perceived leverage in cushy places can be financially mitigated by a really good attorney, but you can't buy a return to better times and whole relationships.

Men of a certain age have tough changes to face, manage, and accept. A few of us just make middle-age much harder than it should be by losing focus on a very short list of top priorities… not to mention those little vows to God and others.

Dads, if you do nothing else, leave your empowered kids the valuable lessons of leverage and how to use it wisely or not at all.
Most of all, good times and not so, future adults are watching, listening, and learning from every big decision we make through our middle years.
God's speed getting through them well, fellow guys, and here's to growing very old with that one true love you never lost."

He had given up on lots of things and unreliable people and places too… add another to the list…elections and historic revisionism….

"2000 redux. No joke. Sad."

"Is this 2012 or 2000? Twelve years wasted by two guys I voted for. I gave up today. No vote. That's my privilege. My passport is ready…

I'm proud of the fact that I've pretty much stopped watching all cable news shows and all the minions that derive from those

shows. I've even enjoyed my own personal ban on watching the political conventions over the summer and presidential debates this fall.

It may just be that I'm tired of the "take our country back" thing. Are Americans really trying to take this country back from something evil or are we trying to take this country back in time? It's another rhetorical question.

However, I'm going to give the rhetoric a shot. I won't give evil any credibility in this blog. No evil people rule our country right now. Just people. That's all. Just human beings. Flawed as they may be. Thus, let's take a look at taking America back in time, to a much better time and place.

I can only assume that we want to look at the last 100 years or so and not prior to that. I think that the indoor plumbing, less disease, really good life spans, & lower infant mortality century is probably the best place to start.

Do we want to take America back to the horse and buggy era? Probably not. Henry Ford knew what he was doing. What about the Roaring Twenties with that fun, free loving, drinking, just do what feels right time…in other words, the 1990's. Both decades experienced great economic times, great fun and faux wealth generated, and a huge bubble that was about to pop in a very big way. Shall we go there again? How about the thirty's and forty's with the Great Depression and World War 2? We call those folks the greatest generation for good reason. No joking there. Do we possibly want to take America back to those significant challenges?

Hey, the 1950's! That was a time of peace and prosperity the likes we will probably never know again! Oh, but, let's think about our children huddled under their school desks trying to fend off a nuclear holocaust. really? The Cold War probably did make people shiver just a bit. No thanks.

Oh, but those swingin' early JFK 1960's…love songs and cigarettes and booze…you know, the Rat Pack thing. classic. The kind of era that leads to fantastic liver disease, hearty melanoma, lung cancer, and, worst of all, an excess of ex-wives to torture us.

No thanks.

Baby Boomer alert!   Do you remember that America of the late 1960's & early 1970's and, really, all through the depressing 1970's?   Failure of real leadership was all around us, plus high interest rates, gas lines, plus terrible economic conditions… and….disco. Need I go on?

The next decade was my favorite. Actually, it still is my favorite…if looking backwards is healthy. Ronald Reagan was the grandfather I never had. He was a hero to me as a child and still is as a middle age man today.   That very decade may never be repeated, since we just don't have any leader right now who can bring opposing sides together for a consensus and actually move America forward in a constructive and fiscally responsible way. Much like the 1920's, the 1990's came with huge growth, explosion of faux wealth, and then a big ol' bubble that just had to pop!   But, enough about Monica Lewinsky. Let's talk about the 2000's.

"Help is on the way!" That was the sign that was in my yard through the 2000 election process and even through those 42 days or so I remember into December, as we couldn't figure out who our next   president would be….yikes, what a decade that followed. Past justifiably blowing up a country that attacked us, we went into a war that really wasn't necessary. And we've lost thousands, if not tens of thousands of lives, in the process of senseless war. Is that the America we want to take back? Now, here we are. Hope & Change, part deux. Re-elect Prez No Hope …or…elect Prez No Change.   That is our choice, it seems.

I do believe that I will take door number 3, Monty! (1970's game show reference, y'all). I simply choose not to vote for either guy. I know. I know. Many men and women have died for my right to vote. However, I see any sacrifice on my behalf as simply offering me the ability to not vote, if I so choose.   That, my friends, is real freedom.

I have no desire to take America back from anyone, anything, nor any ideal that we imagine was better than where we are today. I just have a remarkable desire for my kids to grow up happy and healthy… and for anyone, who wants to find their new America,   wherever that be… in Central America, South America, or the America we all know here in North America…to each his or her own.

Rest assured, there's no taking back of America in any way, shape, or form. America is always a work in progress. 236 years of remarkable performance, lacking, succeeding, starving, thriving, and whatever else you want to throw at it… and here we are. No one leader can possibly fix what ails us, as a nation. There are hundreds needed to seek consensus in Washington DC. There are thousands more in state capitals all across America. And millions of Citizens who can make real things happen for real change. It's not about 1 guy in the White House.

This first Tuesday in November, 2012, will have no effect on the destiny of America. The Destiny of America is determined by its people. And its people can find its own America in its own little home towns or somewhere in some country of Central America or whatever America you wanna make wherever you want to make it.   Horace Greeley said "Go West, young man", way back in the day. But, today, it's go wherever life takes you, young man. Go find your freedom, wherever it maybe. Go find your success, wherever it maybe. Go find your love, life, and pursuit of happiness for your family wherever it may be, young and not so.

Let's not take America back to anything. Let's just take our own America, whatever that may be, to a much better place. God's speed. God's speed, to you all…wherever He may lead you."

Lots of time on his hands. Lots of thoughts too. Then, darn that dream…

"Dreams seem pretty real to me…"

"Just a dream, I keep telling myself. Or was it?   So rhetorical. Dad & I were in some living room just chatting about memories, comparing notes about Maui, Scottsdale, and family trips with our kids and those many family beach weeks over four decades. Dad was all smiles and offered great detail about fun times that were void of work and the mundane. That's about it for what I recall. Almost…

I woke up pretty abruptly last night in tears. Yes, this middle-age guy woke up crying. Pillow was damp. What the hell? Yes, Dad is dying a slow, miserable death. Weaker everyday, it seems. I get it. Or, do I?

Our bodies send us mental signals all day and maybe even at night. Maybe God is telling me something. Maybe I'm being challenged to be a better Dad than I know. Maybe I'm making all of this up. Maybe not.

What is certain is that My Love & I have 4 brilliant kids, two grown girls and two little dudes, and their genetics are set. It's only my love, behavior, and counsel left to help all four along their respective journeys. I hope none of them awake in tears, due to my journey, memories, or counsel, nor anyone else's.

On second thought, maybe those were tears of joy for the good to great times Dad & I did enjoy. Maybe. We'll see what tonight brings.

Sweet dreams to you this Season."
But, the dreams of the Season turned into nightmares

"Did God die last week?"

" Rhetorical query of today: Is there any chance that God is gone? Did He exit before 9/11/01? Did it happen last week? Or sometime in-between? Or…is He just up there letting free-will do its thing in horrific ways?

What really happened this past Friday morn in Newtown, CT is beyond my comprehension, as a father of 4…2 of which are the age or so of the 20 kids & souls lost this week.

God seems to be absent yet again. Is He angry at America? The world? Those who love the most innocent around us?   Or, like the 2nd amendment of our Constitution, does unadulterated

freedom and/or free-will come with inevitable tragedy too?

From huge towers of NYC, to a movie theater in CO, to malls and schools all over America & the world…where is the One who can smite at-will? I'm as confused as ever.

Very fitting that today is a gloomy, rainy Sunday. One that I found myself weeping yet again on my morning walk and later watching, of all things, a very appropriate and dignified opening to the NFL pregame show on ESPN. Reminding fans about 20 innocent children, ages 6 or 7. And 6 adults who were murdered too. I know no one in CT and I am still aching in waves. I have no clue how one feels in Newtown, CT. No clue.

Is God still around? Did He ache about this? Did He allow this as another "lesson" for us? Again, I have no clue. I'm just sad and confused…and very grateful for our 4 beautiful and brilliant kids of 20, 19, 8, & 6.

Tell a child how smart and loved he or she is today.   Hug a loved child of yours today. Protect a child
from real-life horror stories today. Ask God for a little inspiration, a little hope, just a little clue into
what we should do moving forward….assuming that He is still there and ready to help.

But, we all know what happens when we assume, now more than ever.
May God Bless you & yours this remaining Season of Christmas 2012 & beyond….
Please, God, give us all a clue and blessings to all who ache this Season. Please.”

**His year of 2013 chugged on, with 3 lost loved-ones and one new love
came on-board. He learned to sail and virtually met dozens of sailors and
sailing families online. He even began building his research for sailing
blogs, boats to look for someday, and where to sail and live someday. He
was and still is dead serious. Sail the Caribbean during high-season,
eventually chartering one or more boats, and then sail north to the Keys,
the Gulf, and up the eastern seaboard to Maine for the holidays. The
plan is a work in progress, but here's his first written lunge at his new
vision for their second-half of living…**

"One particular harbor…"

"it's been quite a…summer?" is part of a live "Come Monday" song from Jimmy Buffett in Hawaii.

I highly recommend his Pandora channel for a getaway anywhere. Yes, it has been quite a summer.
Usual trips with kids, lots of sun, never enough beach time. The usual. But, this summer turned another
page on us. We said goodbye to my Dad. He went on his own terms after just a three-day hospital stay.
It was time. Alzheimer's disease did not have its way. Neither did diabetes. Dad did. He did not want to
live under an oxygen mask. So, he removed it for the last time and he left us. On his terms. "My Way"
as Sinatra would sing. Good for you, Dad.

Life does indeed go on. Saying goodbye to three loved ones this year should be enough. I hope God
agrees. Losing both of our Dads this year is awfully sad. But, both suffer no more and Heaven is a
funnier place now with them.

Fall is in the air around here. Perfect running, biking, camping, & sailing weather is upon us. Really
looking forward to sharing a family weekend with our girls at there university next weekend. Then, a
sailing camp reunion for our family the next weekend. And I just booked our fall stay up at Elkmont in
the GSM National Park and ordered our Big Agnes tent, as well. Should be crisp & cozy up the
mountains. Then, before we know it, the holidays will be here. Time does fly.

Back to that "One particular harbor", sing…I found it. Actually, I found a few marinas. In a few years,
we will be blogging & entertaining friends, family, and tourists from one of several harbors &
coastlines between St. Pete, Florida and the Florida Keys. After securing my keelboat certification, my
next task is to secure my coastal cruising & SCUBA certs, then, work towards my Captain's license, in
order to make a living with fun, sun, sand, & saltwater. It's how our second-half needs to be enjoyed.

Give our boys an adventure. Give our girls a fun destination, as their schedules allow. Prep ourselves for our empty nest time, probably on a Hake-Seaward 46′ in the BVI. And, as for grandkids…well, they'll have a ball. Lots to do, one step at a time. If this year has reaffirmed anything for me, it's my passion to do it "My Way". Not any banker's way. Not any workaholic's way. Not any preacher's way. Not any politician's way. My way. Clutter free, downsized, quality over quantity, and paying cash for everything moving forward. My way, with my one true Love. as Buffett would

harbors & quality

With our four true loves and their partners & kids to come. Our way.
Let the training continue. I just started today running at least

10k in just over one hour. Heart started fluttering a bit again. That little thing began the day after Dad died. But, I'm fine. I'm here. I'm healthier now at 45 than I was in my lucrative 30's. Ginny is too. She's one hot Mom. Let the training & execution of The Plan continue.

Lastly, many thanks to fellow writers at WindTraveler.net , ZeroToCruising.com ,LahoWind.com, sv-Totem, The Monkey's Fist, & Savannah Sails for a tremendous sailing & live aboard education.

Keeping it real, they are. And inspirational too.
Sail on…to that one particular harbor, y'all."

Sailing is, yet again, another metaphor for life. Life is great in fair winds and sunshine.
Then, if turns when a squall blows through, let alone a cat 5 hurricane. He knows that they will need a community there. Many communities in many places around the sailing world. Those communities make solutions to various boating problems come much quicker and cheaper. He understands that and their new life will come "in God's time". Lesson learned.
When the wind stops, just be still and wait. His wind will be there or you enjoy the stillness, which is rare, just like in the real world.

He and his Love are now the new patriarch and even matriarch, even

with both of their moms still around. They are in charge of taking this family forward, leading the way, and welcoming all kids and grandkids who will follow. Only time will tell…God's time, of course.

Their girls have their own future plans to return to Spain, Panama, Germany, etc. and maybe live, love, and work there. Maybe California, too. Who knows? It's their lives, not his nor his Love nor their other family's. It's very exciting. He wants to stay flexible to go to and not miss out on their lives for months or years at a time. Thank God they are all very interested in western Europe and other culturally rich parts of the world.

He wanted to explore the world more than ever and this adds fuel to that internal fire…

"Boobs, Bubba, & wrestling"

"As this school year began, I ran into an old acquaintance and he was nice enough to introduce me to his wife.
The intro was unique, but not unexpected. "Brad's the one that would write letters to the Editor…or you used to…". So true. Like pressed khakis, dress clothes, crowded parties, wine coolers, bleached jeans, and relying on anyone for financial advice, I've given up on productive politics and the hacks & puppeteers who manage their every move. Public and private airing of opinion has zero impact without a checkbook whipped out for results desired.
I've learned this cynical truth in various forms from a majority of elected "leaders". The sad reality is local, regional, and, most disappointing, nationwide with our Congress, which is primarily comprised of bullies or lemmings. Clean house again next year and a new crop of each will emerge. The historic tradition of compromise & reconciliation is dead. The Gipper & Tip must be rolling over these days. Reagan offered amnesty to 3 million illegal aliens, sense he was a realistic person and bigger leader. This White House & Congress set up epic annual battles with unrealistic budgets, trillion $+ annual deficits, and inevitable debt-ceiling wrestling matches. Today's politics is more like a sport. Winners, losers, and fans cheering on each sideline. But, a football analogy would be too kind.
Today's politics here in our hometown, in our state house, and in DC resembles professional wrestling more than any sport. Neckties replace masks. Nice suits replace tights. Past that, its the very same egos, testosterone fueled angst, and an endless search

for ultimate domination in our politics. Not results. Not greater good. Not sacrifice of any sort. Just re-election. That's the perpetual goal of most elected officials.

Our federal government hit the mat yesterday and each opponent is blaming the other for throwing the good fight. Sad, but typical.

It's no wonder why so many other countries look so much more healthy & positive for frustrated Americans and ex-pats. After a year of research, I've realized that there are far more healthy places to call home someday.

This week has proven again why a few banana republics offer greater economic & political stability than our birthright of a country.

Where are our Gippers & Tip O'Neils of today…dead and long gone, it seems. Cheers."

Enough about politics. Scratch that one off the list too. He even stopped voting altogether, after 2008. He's focused beyond America, planning trips, and just caring for the greatest loves of his life…simple, big priorities…

"Growing up vs. Giving up"

"You gotta love a great sunset. The metaphors abound in my mind.
At our middle age, sunsets take on very different meanings. Our parents sunsets. Our kids' childhood sunsets. Our

professional & personal friendship sunsets. If you're as reflective as I am, you see sunsets as our new normal.

Every month, it seems, we experience one or more personal sunsets of friends marriages. It's a generational thing.
Our folks persevered. Same careers. Same home. Same friends. Same vacations. Same & predictable. But, they made it through decades of triumphs & maybe tragedy.
Our GenX is different. The 7 year itch seems to be stretched a bit to a decade or two. Careers get stagnant. Organized religion loses its luster. Healthy relationships grow fewer. And love is shared more sparingly with those who matter the most. I know. I'm a poster boy for all of the above.
Fortunately, at my age, I'm more than a little obsessed about where we are & where we are going as a family over the next few decades. It seems that my success & struggles of my 20's & very lucrative & excessive 30's & leaner, meaner, and healthier 40's have tee'd me and our family up for a killer 50's and beyond. That forward obsession is my largest time & energy ROI for the time I have remaining in this realm.
My Love is healthy. Our four kids are relatively healthy. Two are globe-trotters and two will be someday. And, I'm literally collecting volumes of research about cultures & destinations for our family to visit, play, work, & live someday. Think about a triangle between St. Champlain, Vermont. That's how & where we need to grow up as a family. That's The Plan. Family love & very close friends.
All that really matters, while we sail this big, blue wet thing.
Cheers & happy sailing, all."
Pete, Florida & Tortola, BVI & Lake

Their long winter plodded along, as they really looked forward to the fun spring and summer months to come, which is a reminder of living somewhere where it's spring and summer year-round.

He's mentally checked out of his hometown and, thankfully, so has his Love. The future plans are now in motion and they will be leaving in a year or two, as planned. In the meantime, he's got two little dudes to train to be real men, real husbands, and real fathers someday…

"Guy talk."

"These little guys. Little men in training, if you will. Love 'em.
Today is a big day. Shouldn't be. But, it is. Dad says so.
Today is another first. A conversation my Dad never had with me. Of course, my Dad never told me that he loved me… in those exact words…which I, in turn, tell each boy daily at school drop-off and at bedtime. Gotta break some family cycles, you know. But, I digress.
Today is the day for my first ever "i know school sucks for you" conversation. It's like work for most adults. It's just what you must do…or think you must do. Your real interests in life don't matter at school or work. It's just what you do.
Do the Core work. Take the Core tests. Please the teacher, who needs to please the Principal, who needs to please the System, that needs to please the Governor, who could care a less about pleasing the federal government.
We're farming little tester seeds. Not good, but it's the norm.
Why today? Well, this morn was the third Monday in a row where one or both boys pretended to be ill. Monday blahs, which we all get, were not going to work today. And, I'm done.
It's time for our first Guy Talk. I'm sitting both down to explain how I did not enjoy the conformity of school. How I loathed many parts of school. How I was a terrible athlete, so I played golf. But, how I embraced more social subjects, loved just being near cute girls, and how I found myself leading over time and not following my contemporaries past 7th grade.
Spencer Tracy, I'm not. But, I do admire his classic work on film. To me, "Guess Who's Coming to Dinner" is the greatest American film ever. It's about New vs status-quo. Old vs young. And, yes, racial divides. Most of all, it's about a positive evolution of our thinking about our very real world. Of course, we don't have that movie scenario to discuss here today…but we do have a real divide to address head-on…and we will. Guy Talk is my conversation brand idea. Thoughts?
God be with us. God be with you & yours. God bless us….everyone."

Time continues to fly, as he fast-approached his 48th year, and a summer full of fun. A summer of traditions on the Gulf, boys growth through camping, he and his Love's renewal in Costa Rica, and even his transformation on the Camino de Santiago, Spain. They planned and executed his best summer of his life. It's been a soulsearching few years. Three plus years void of organized religion, except for Christmas and Easter. We all have traditions.

This would-be Captain has been writing his first book, in two of our son's notebooks. He thought it apropos to revisit his childhood in a Cars/Lightening McQueen notebook and early adulthood in an Angry Birds notebook.

Granted, this rough, very rough draft will be edited many ways and put on-line eventually. He struggled with self-publishing, which seems to work for the sultry Meredith Wild books, but may or may not work for this first novella of its kind.

Big summer times were ahead as they head to the Gulf with all 4 kids, no grandparents, plus one boyfriend.

Most of all, he's Looking forward to his greatest adventure ever, hiking the Camino de Santiago of Spain with his oldest daughter and then off to a well-deserved, allinclusive get-away to Costa Rica with his Love… her…

In July 2015, he changed forever. Thanks, Camino. This is the Camino, The Way, & his renewal.

That's when he left this writer. He was my oldest friend and he was my oldest enemy. He went to Spain with his daughter and he left me forever. I won't miss him.

I'm still conflicted, happy most often, not depressed as before, and very resigned to my fate as the best husband, father, and semi-retired whatever I can be.
God blessed me.

The Camino sure seemed to, as, well, which is based on the The Way of St. James. The apostle & brother of Jesus, who made his way, as legend has it, to Santiago de Compostela by boat after being martyred back in Jerusalem. Yes, his body was set sail and the wind of angels carried him to that corner of Spain. A pilgrimage grew for hundreds of years and fell off when Europe became to dangerous to travel alone on foot. The tradition picked up hundreds of years later with the enlightened era of Europe and really took off in the 1960's. 2015 will see over 300,000 pilgrimages finish their individual journeys.

Fast forward almost 47 years for me, and, there I was with my daughter flying across the pond to Madrid, taking the train to Leon, then a cab to their Albergue and we begin to soak up the local culture immediately.

My oldest daughter had just achieved her Masters in Education, specifically ESL focused, and she wanted a memorable and meaningful trip with her old dad. And, shot got it. She was a wonderful translator too.

It was a magical, sweaty hike. Northern Spain, in July, is nice and cool each morning and night, but gets hot by the time your daily hike is done. We began around 7am each day and were done by Noon or 1pm, never past 2pm, and we covered 15k-25k per day, with two days over 30k (tough!). We had the most popular guide book and jumped ahead to albergues and pensions that were in smaller villages, just past the recommended towns.

I discovered and fell in love with a lifestyle that seemed to be the antitheses of my homeland. These new friends, pilgrims and hosts alike, lived a simple, sun-soaked life. Simple, delicious food. Light breakfasts. Lots of meat & cheese later. Local vino tinto and Spainish cervesas, por favor. Work a little early, take a long lunch/siesta , and return to work and eat a late meal before retiring for the night. No tv's? I loved that. It was surreal , like blending vacation time into every workday. 7 days a week of relaxation, a lot of great food and drink, and a little productivity. It is a wonderful balance of work, conversation, relaxation, and productivity. Something that is hard to find in the New World. They really live.

Our first night was a culinary orgy with small plates of food offered with every cervesa. By their third stop, we found ourselves at the house of Jamon Jamon. Yes, so nice, they named it twice. Order cervesa, por favor, and the free Iberian ham, bread, and cheeses will flow your way. Tiny place, but huge flavors. Every stop setting them back a few euros each. 20 euros or so later, we were stuffed with food, beer, memories, and a desire to return to Leon, Spain someday. A must, it seemed to us. Now, that's impressive!

Of course, reality kicked in and someone decided that this beautiful cathedral won't open to pilgrims until 9:30am, when most hit The Way around sunrise or 7am then. We were just a bit excited.

Each hike was a new adventure with new sights, new historical monuments, and new towns with nice people offering "Buen Camino" at every turn, as other pilgrims would as well over the entire journey.

There were singles, retired folks, couples, and even families of all ages. Everyday was a literal adventure with a varying cast of characters and a different destination every day and night. Life could not be more interesting.

Kids singing on The Way was a beautiful thing.
So was making new friends on the first night, the second, and on and on. Then, we met my South African equal, Larry, Miss Britta, and our favorite hosts on night two.

Another first…being in the minority and I loved it. First of all, not too many dad-daughter pairs. Not to many 6' 3", 270lb guys out there either. Europeans are smaller, thinner, and healthier, it seemed, from observing a few hundred along The Way.

Best of all, there were only a few Americans...like 5, that we met over those weeks. Spain, France, Germany, Italy, and Canada covered 97% of who we met, including a kiwi or two. Most were multi-lingual and communication by voice and/or hand signals and pointing worked very well too. It also helped to know a few key words and to be that polite, and not so loud, American. I think that got me through The Way very well, when my personal translator was not by my side, except with these fun ladies of Spain...

It just kept getting better. One day at a time. One tiny hamlet to somewhat historic village at a time. It's what we did every day for over two weeks. Moreover, we did not see a drop of rain during the entire Camino experience. It was, again, magical, in more ways than one. God was...

....everywhere.

Everywhere.

We started out walking 15-20k a day, picked up the pace to 20-25k a day and went over 30k two days of The Way. That was our maximum and required even more vino tinto and delicious food to relax. For my frugal friends out there, once you get past the plane ticket, everything on the Camino is very affordable to just cheap. From 89 cent deodorant to 1-2 euro bottles of vino tinto to full meals with vino for 8-10 euros pp per diner. Or, you could shop the local market or "Supermercado" for all you need to snack, cook, and share with others. Cheap! Most pilgrims aren't rich and neither are the villagers of Northern Spain. Sure, there are 5-star hotels in the bigger towns of Leon, Astorga, and even Santiago…and Madrid is a huge, expensive metropolis…but you can still buy things cheap in the neighborhood Supermercado. No big box stores, strip malls, car lots, malls, movie theatres, nor fast-food chains anywhere in sight on The Way.

The Way is all about nature, conversations, reflection, and discovery, religious and otherwise. We joined others every night at either a private Aubergue (never the crowded and sketchy municipal ones) or a private pension for as little as 10 euros per night for both of us, but mostly 20-30 euros (cash) per night. We splurged a couple of nights when village pickings were slim and lived in luxury for 55 euros a night.
They were worth it and one included a big breakfast the next day…and our host did our laundry!

This was our sweet host and my lovely, translating daughter.
Clean clothes are a big deal on the dusty, sweaty Camino and she took
great care of us a few days in. Others did too. Showing us to the market.
Feeding us. Caring for a rare blister…at the dinner table…that was
quite a night. Serving us the most affordable everything we needed.
Selling me earplugs for my daughter…but, I don't snore!?

One day and one open range and one village and one meal at a time, I
changed for the better, thanks to my daughter and her desire to do this
with her old dad.

Did I mention how cheap everything is on the Camino? Yes? Well, it is.
We ate simply from tortillas (egg and potato ommlette/quiche dish) to
croissant & butter to jamon, cheese, and bread to pulpo (octopus grilled

or simmered in sauce, over potatoes).

Other creative dishes were available when we stayed in bigger villages or pensions with restaurants, which were common too. Again, you set your budget of maybe 10-15 euro's a day and you will eat and drink just fine…

Gorgeous scenery, lovely European people, delicious food & drink, and great exercise of mind and body… …that is The Way of the Camino de Santiago, whether you haul it for 5 weeks from France and cover 800kms or if you take the time you have and about three weeks to fly there, start in Leon, Spain, and cover 300km to Santiago. It was my longest stretch away from home and my first trip to Europe. Great call, oldest daughter. So was staying in the hippie pensions, which are usually vegetarian…but, amazing vegetarian for this meat-lover.

Three or four courses and pitchers of vino tinto flows

all evening. Dinner at 7 sharp. 9 euros each…cash.

Oh, and there's no tipping… anywhere. None. It's an insult to their profession, whatever it may be. NO TIPPING! Your meal, room, or whatever cost is relatively cheap and somehow covers the pay

of servers and anyone in any business where tipping is standard back home. It took time to get used to, at least one minute, and I was home there too. And, there's cake for breakfast! And, combo laundry and octopus house…never saw that coming in this idilic village.

We came to the last 100km to Santiago…

… and it was the realization that there were only a few days left to go. Missing those at home, but not missing my hometown at all. This experience just reaffirmed my need to grab the kids and my Love and hitting the road, flying away, just changing e v e r y t h i n g … a n d w e a r e planning to do just that.

And, now for something ridiculous…..a selfie portfolio.

We made it to Santiago. Lots more to tell about that last 100k, including the place we stayed with a pool, tiki bar, and lots of pilgrims in bikinis and swim trunks. Roughing it poolside, after a long day's walk in Galicia. There's also lots to tell about Santiago.

But, I'll let the pictures do that for me…

She's trying to kill me!

Then came the last weekend in Madrid with my youngest daughter, who took a break from her time in Germany to join us.

We returned home and to Germany, respectively, and I, again, will never be the same. The world is so much bigger than that of my childhood, of my young business career, and far bigger than anyone who grew up here were intended to imagine. I appreciate the creative class and the explorers of the world now more than ever. I appreciate Europe and its people more than I ever could without immersing myself in one little corner of that continent. I cannot imagine how many places of Spain, Italy, France, and the Greek Islands there are left to explore with my Love and one or more of our kids. I pray that our little dudes are as big at exploring the world as their sisters are…here they are welcoming me home.

I'm very blessed. I know that. I love that. And, I am loved by the most loved people in my life. And, we have big plans ahead. More traveling… more books to write…maybe an unorthodox Camino Frances travel guide and more…who knows where my second half of life goes.

I just know that it will go. Life will go on. It's just a matter of what we do
with it and how we share it with new communities and, especially, our
kids now and grandkids to come.
When they come, we will be ready and they will have great experiences
with us.

Lastly, thanks again to the Love of my life and all others who have put
up with me and to all who all who have enjoyed this love story of one boy
growing up to be a

middle-age man. Love and many blessings to you all from me and my
Love…

Do you think you might want to hike the Camino? Let me help you, por favor.

Just read. Read a year before. Read that entire year. Read on the plane.
I bought four of the best books I thought Amazon could produce and
each offered good to great advice. The best, by far, was the upbeat,
practical, and even mystical back-pocket sized book of all Camino
books…

Looks a little rough. You bet. If I wore you out for two weeks straight,
you might not look too good either. This was my Camino bible.

Next, what to pack. Quick dry shirts (Patagonia & Mtn Harware), same
in shorts (Columbia , Marmot, Mtn Harware, Patagonia), and
underwear (Ex-officio works the best). Just 2-4 of each depending on
your laundry accessibility. I took 5 of everything , which was too much.
Lesson learned. Oh, and hankies. It's our family thing. But, I used a lot

of handkerchiefs on the Camino. A sun blocking Columbia hat too.
Where did all of my stuff go???

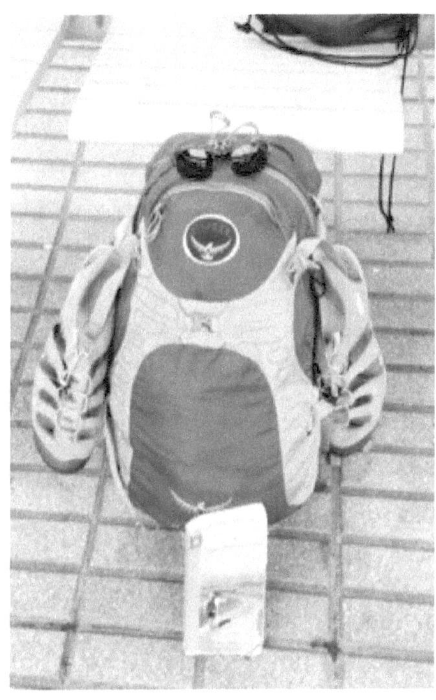

My Osprey 24liter backpack. Light, compact, fits easily on planes and
trains. Held more than I needed for the Camino, plus strapped a water
bottle, my back-up Keens, and a bottle opener to it. No problem.

No trekking poles for me. Too noisy. Not physically helpful to me. Just
adding tap dancing to a peaceful hike. Most important items of all:

Great wool socks (SmartWool or Wigwam, my choice) that may claim to
be "blister-free"..and they almost were. But those dry socks with these
tough, waterproof Keens…

Your winning combination.

No running. Just walking and hiking. Unless, cervesas are up ahead.

Sure, bring all of the toiletries you think you need, but my toothbrush, floss, comb, gel, soap, shampoo, quickdry towel , and deodorant all fit nicely.

Bring plenty of euros and your wifi capable smartphone and you will be set, with Camino bible as your ultimate guide to each day's landmarks & destinations.

Lastly, bring a best friend or loved one to share this journey with and remember forever. I've been on Daddaughter adventures to our known places of NYC and Passa-Grille, but never two weeks plus into the unknown. If you just want to be alone, I guess it's possible. Come to the Camino alone and you will meet a wide spectrum of characters, 99% well-educated Spaniards, French, German, Italian, or Canadian. We Americans are rarely seen or heard on the Camino, at least during our two weeks in July. And it was wonderful. One retired steel mill fella from Ohio, who strongly resembled Santa Claus, was the loudest person at each cafe' stop. His vast knowledge of everything reminded me of my Dad.

Go do it, if you like. Alone or not, you'll never really be alone. You will be with various "pilgrims" as you go.
As the song says, you will never walk alone, at least on the Camino.
Our Camino proved it.
For more prep, laughs & mostly true things about the Camino (we had no bladder issues) check this out:
http://matadornetwork.com/notebook/20-truths-walkingcamino-de-santiago/

Hope all of this helps. Go explore. If you can affordably get to France or Spain, do 100km, 300km (like us from Leon to Santiago), or the entire 800km from St. Jean.

You will be challenged and probably glad you did.
Just travel. Wherever you go.
Cheers and Buen Camino! In conclusion...I promise...
My Love gave me a gift last night...the end of this book.

I loathe falling into a Venus vs. Mars argument, yet again. However, I've given up on arguing, as I have given up on many things. Arguing with your Love is about as futile as it gets.

I have an educated guess that most women would be happy to thrilled with a full-time husband, dad, cook, cleaner, launderer, shuttle driver, and grocery shopper... plus son and son-in-law, when needed. I'm also guessing that 99% of my fellow middle-age men out there could not handle my daily chores, even with ample time everyday to read, exercise, listen to smart podcasts, and relax, as well. I enjoy 2-3 hours of speed-walking, weather permitting, on our boulevard everyday. That's 10-15k a day, for health reasons and to keep up for my next pilgrimage. I also do something that my Love, Venus, does not understand. As opposed to seeing a shrink or my MD and getting a drug or two to allow me get through each day, I self-medicate via perfectly legal and almost safe drink. It takes the edge off everyday and I am able to move on.

It also allows me to write things that I may not have otherwise. Many men, much more accomplished than me, did and do the same thing. Ah, remember those three martini lunches…in the middle of the workday? They did happen in enlightened places around the globe. Siestas too. They still happen today. Countless leaders and creative types were able to numb the pain and/or just get a little more creative, as they reach out for their legal drug of choice. Churchill stood his ground and helped save the world with a drink & a cigar in his hand most of each day.

Moreover, I can never be a prosperous/well-known writer, as Hunter S. Thompson, Ernest Hemingway, etc., but I promise those I know and love that I won't end up like them. I'm not tormented anymore. Just disappointed in myself, elated by the success of my Love and our kids, and motivated to write, sail, and sell fun again someday.

I just need this time right now to take care of family business, take care of certain needs by myself, and accept my current lot in life, until our situation changes. I must be healthy and sane for the next entrepreneurial endeavor to come, let alone grandkids and other surprises.

We all have a long time to go. Mars is doing my best, maybe to the chagrin of Venus. I cannot help that. It's who I am right now and I plan to write more, take more sailing courses, build up a network & connected communities in beautiful, sunny places, and eventually land that business opportunity on beautiful water and in full-service marinas where people are happy, connected, and offer great family adventures.

I have, although, made a really big change for me. I'm in my own form of detox from my decade-long drug of choice…lemon-peel infused, 5-times distilled, French vodka. Yep, the good and very affordable drug. I woke up the other night with a dream, maybe even a vision, sweating profusely in a cool room. My mind was racing and I started to recall that it was the exact Tuesday, 10 years ago, that our dear friends', JB and Gina, remains and plane wreckage were found. And, I prayed for God's help for the first time in a long while. The sweating stopped. I cooled off and I then decided to give up my drink of choice, even after enjoying a couple of well-made martinis with my Love just that previous afternoon, while out for an impromptu date. I'm sure that I will enjoy more someday, like a rare taste for filet of beef…but not daily and all-nightly anymore. I have deduced that I am returning to the Camino daily, in my mind, and I'm becoming a reformed European in American skin.

Vino tinto and an occasional cervesa are my drugs of choice again and I hope we return to Spain & Europe to live!

It is my sincere hope that you will come along via my blog, books, websites, and, hopefully, in-person on the Camino and on a really nice catamaran somewhere between Florida and the Caribbean islands, too. We have a long way to go for our family to get there, but we will get there.

Whatever your faith is, keep it. Whatever your lot in life is, try to move forward. Whatever your age, that just does not matter. If you self-medicate yourself, I'm right there with you. Keep it in check. Do what you need to do for you and yours. You'll go nuts otherwise or you'll just be someone else's puppet. Let's not be puppets past those young, adult years that we just had to see through.

Likewise, don't strive to be the puppet-master either. Just be. Be safe alone. Be safe with those you adore.
Just be. As the cliche' says, Life is short.
Yes, it can be.
And, it can be long and exhausting, too.

Do what you need to do to make it pleasant and enjoyable more than not. That's what I'm doing and I don't expect anyone to completely understand.

Thanks, My Love, for this ending, for our beginning, for all in-between, and for all that is to come.
I do love you. Cheers.